The Essential Poets

❖

FUTURE VOLUMES
WILL INCLUDE

The Essential Byron

The Essential Wyatt

The Essential Hardy

The Essential Tennyson

The Essential Browning

The Essential Milton

The Essential Marvell

The Essential Donne

❖

John Donne

BORN   JANUARY–JUNE 1572
DIED   31 MARCH 1631

The Essential
DONNE

Selected and with an
Introduction by
AMY CLAMPITT

The Ecco Press
New York

Introduction and selection copyright © 1988 by Amy Clampitt
All rights reserved
Published in 1988 by The Ecco Press
26 West 17th Street, New York, N.Y. 10011
Published simultaneously in Canada by
Penguin Books Canada Ltd., Ontario
Printed in the United States of America
Designed by Reg Perry

FIRST EDITION

Library of Congress Cataloging-in-Publication Data

Donne, John 1572-1631.
The Essential Donne
selected and with an introduction by Amy Clampitt.—1 ed.
p.   cm.—(The Essential poets; 8)
I. Clampitt, Amy   II. Title.
III. Series: Essential poets (New York, N.Y.); 8.
PR2246.C52   1988   821'.3—dc19   88-24394

ISBN 0-88001-206-4 (pbk.)

Portrait of John Donne
by an unknown artist, 1620.
The Deanery, St. Paul's Cathedral.
By courtesy of the Dean of St. Paul's.

Contents

❖

For Stuart Gerry Brown

The Essential Donne

Introduction

❖❖

Half a century has passed since T. S. Eliot wrote, at the tercentenary of the death of John Donne, "We probably understand sympathetically Donne to-day better than poets and critics fifty years hence will understand him." If the phrasing sounds uncomfortable, it's no wonder. Not quite twenty years before, Eliot had made some pronouncements that are still quoted, and that had much to do with the recent high repute of Donne, among others of his time. In 1926 Eliot had given some lectures on Donne, but chose not to turn them into a book. By 1931, the tercentenary year, he was clearly in the process of backing off. His initial fervor—"A thought to Donne was an experience; it modified his sensibility. When a poet's mind is perfectly equipped for its work, it is constantly amalgamating disparate experiences"—had evaporated; now he was saying that in Donne, "learning is just information suffused with emotion, or combined with emotion not essentially relevant to it." Behind the squinting contortion of that forecast was no boast of superior sympathy but the squirm of embarrassment: times change, and thinking falls all over itself.

Such thinking, however evanescent, is the stuff of literary reputation. Milton and Wordsworth have had their undoubted, if less febrile, ups and downs. In the early 1940s the poems of Donne were still very much in fashion, and I myself absorbed what Helen Gardner saw in retrospect as the pervasive (if never explicitly stated) notion that "Donne was a more interesting and significant poet than Milton." But the pervasiveness of that notion may say more about a generation's vendetta against epic size than about Donne himself. Milton is no longer execrated; Wordsworth has come very near to being trendy; any day now, epic sublimity in English may be approached with something other than an involuntary sigh.

And what of Donne, half a century after Eliot's own second thoughts? If he is no longer trendy, neither has he been relegated anywhere—even though in the latest major study, *John Donne: Life, Mind and Art* (Oxford University Press, 1981), John Carey does hint at a continuing urge to cut back on the favorable notices. At any rate, Donne is still, as he always has been, controversial—one of those poets toward whose work a sigh or a shrug is barely conceivable. I have read that Borges singled out the lines

> *Licence my roving hands, and let them go*
> *Before, behind, between, above, below.*
> *O my America, my new found land,*

from Donne's elegy "To his Mistress Going to Bed," as a demonstration of his greatness as a poet. C. S. Lewis, no partisan, described this same elegy as merely pornographic. John Carey went further, denouncing it as proof that Donne was a sadist—a conclusion disputed at length by William Empson, on the basis of his reading of a single line; and since there is no way to know which of several variants Donne would finally have preferred, a resolution is unlikely.

Even when Donne's text is not in dispute, both meaning and estimate remain unsettled. Concerning one of the most frequently reprinted of all his poems, "The Ecstasy," the wrangling has been long, vehement, and similarly inconclusive. Coleridge praised it, and so did Pound. For C. S. Lewis, it was arguably a "much nastier" poem than the bedtime elegy. What Donne himself had in mind—seduction by way of Neoplatonic sophistries, or something rather more elevated—would seem by now almost, if not entirely, irretrievable. There is the vocabulary to be dealt with: not only an alchemical term such as *concoction*, but the title word itself is to be approached with caution. When Keats wrote of the nightingale *pouring its soul abroad* "in such an ecstasy," he was using the word with more precision than we generally do. These days, as all currencies are debased, the worst ravages are linguistic—and so we need to be reminded that etymologically an ecstasy is a going forth *(ek-stasis)* and further that in the vocabulary of the Neoplatonists it denoted the going forth of the soul to be united with the object of its desire. Clearly this, and not some more generalized rapture, is Donne's subject; but how much nearer it brings us to the poet's own frame of mind, I am not sure.

Possibly a greater stumbling block than *ecstasy,* a word Donne used rarely, is *soul*—which he mentions so habitually as to be troubling for a twentieth-century reader. Whatever philosophical uncertainties the poet may have been prey to, for him there was no doubt that the soul existed, as genuinely as the corporeal frame itself. He also believed that the sun revolved about the earth—believed it, notwithstanding the Copernican heresy, to which he not infrequently referred, in much the same way that he believed in a deity with power over the human soul. He troubled himself a good deal over theology, as only a believer with an excitable intellect would be inclined to do. It is partly because of this excitability that people discovering Donne for the first time tend to view him as an old poet with surprisingly modern attitudes. Though of late a considerable edifice of critical writing has been built on such misreading, I can't suppose that any of those engaged in the construction (and deconstruction) would say that outright misreading is therefore to be encouraged. And in any event the stumbling block remains: John Donne wrote of the soul as an entity whose existence he did not doubt. This should be clear from the first poem of his ever to appear in print—"The Expiration," published in 1609 with a musical setting by Ferrabosco in a volume of airs. "So, so," it begins, "break off this last lamenting kiss,/ Which sucks two souls, and vapours both away."

Donne's friend and exact contemporary Ben Jonson, who in the familiar lyric beginning "Drink to me only with thine eyes" declared that

The thirst that from the soul doth rise
Doth ask a drink divine

likewise equated the soul with breathing: the wreath of roses his lady had declined to accept, but only sniffed at and sent back again, is declared by the singer to grow and smell "not of itself, but thee." Hyperbole of this sort was rampant at the time, and is of course typical of Donne. An earlier line in the song—"But might I of Jove's nectar sup,/ I would not change for thine"—does, however, suggest a difference between the two poets. The names of Venus, of Mercury, even of Jove, appear now and then in the poems of Donne, but not nearly so often as do saints, heretics, canonizations, and other ecclesiastical paraphernalia; and when Love is personified, it is more likely to be in such terms as "Love, any devil else but you . . ." Unlike Jonson, whose frame of mind may be described as classical, Donne at his most profane is essentially a Christian poet.

He was born in 1572, into a time when theological and political turmoil were even more thornily intertwined than they now are. That same year witnessed the slaughter of French Protestants on the eve of St. Bartholomew, when Donne was only a few months old. The air of Elizabethan England was poisoned by fear of popery; Donne's parents were Catholic; his brother Henry was sent to prison for harboring a Roman priest, and died there. John Donne himself studied at Oxford, and later at Cambridge, but without then taking a degree, since to do so meant subscribing to the Thirty-nine Articles and adhering to the Church of England. The year he was twenty, he was admitted to Lincoln's Inn for the study of law. He appeared around this time as a wit and a worldling, "attentive to ladies and a great frequenter of plays." He must also by then have begun writing verse, which—as was the fashion among young men of that station—circulated in manuscript, but which he disdained to publish. Among the earliest of these poems were probably the satires, whose prevailing note is sounded by the opening lines of Satire 2:

> *Sir; though (I thank God for it) I do hate*
> *Perfectly all this town.*

What has caused his gorge to rise is a bad poet who is also a lawyer—the stereotypical creep, still revoltingly alive and identifiable notwithstanding the Elizabethan attire. That the author is himself a poet and a lawyer only adds to the scathing force of the indictment. At once angry and ambitious, he already knows all about the world:

> *Bastardy abounds not in kings' titles, nor*
> *Simony and sodomy in churchmen's lives,*
> *As these things do in him; by these he thrives.*

At his most forthright, Donne is anything but simple. The text of this satire contains, along with a spate of legalistic expressions, a liberal seasoning of religious ones: papists, confessors, schoolmen, canonists, abbeys, Pater nosters and litanies, Carthusian fasts, the Church Fathers, Luther, even Satan himself are all at hand. What is here implicit the third satire makes explicit: a protracted wrestling within himself concerning "our mistress fair religion"—or, more precisely, the rival claims of the various sects and their spokesmen, clerical and otherwise:

> *Fool and wretch, wilt thou let thy soul be tied*
> *To man's laws, by which she shall not be tried*
> *At the last day? Or will it then boot thee*
> *To say a Philip, or a Gregory,*
> *A Harry, or a Martin taught thee this?*

More than twenty years were to pass before the conflict in his own mind was finally, or anyhow ostensibly, resolved, and Donne made his reluctant entrance into a career in the Church of England. The reluctance was not entirely doctrinal; for all his cynicism about preferments and favorites and hangers-on at Whitehall, a life at court, or diplomacy abroad, was what he had aimed for. In fact, such a career would seem to have been assured: after taking part in two naval expeditions against Spain—to Cadiz in 1596 and to the Azores in the following year—he had become secretary to Sir Thomas Egerton, the lord keeper and an ally of the Earl of Essex. Before long Essex would have angered the queen, turned against her, and been sent to the Tower. He was executed in 1601; but John Donne's own lost prospects had nothing to do with the fortunes of any royal favorite.

Concerning his love affair with his employer's niece, Ann More, their secret marriage, and his dismissal and temporary imprisonment on the charge of violating canon law, we have the facts but hardly any of the flavor, except whatever may incidentally have been preserved in the poems of Donne. The effort to sort out which of these were addressed to his wife, and to just what in their life together they refer, remains inconclusive. Donne was twenty-nine, his wife just sixteen, at the time of their marriage. They lived isolated, dependent on relatives, friends, and literary patrons, in a damp little house at Mitcham in Surrey, where year by year another child arrived, until improving prospects made it possible for them to move to London. There, still in her early thirties, Ann Donne gave birth for the twelfth time. The baby was born dead, and Ann herself died soon after. Whatever else may be said of it, the marriage must often have been overhung with gloom; and if it is assumed that such poems as "Twicknam Garden" and "A Nocturnal upon S. Lucy's Day" were written during the years at Mitcham, their funereal tone is understandable. It is now believed that the Holy Sonnets also date, at least mainly, to this stage of Donne's life, and not to a later one.

By degrees, at any rate, Donne came into favor with the court of James I, and the sometime rake and libertine was known from 1621 onward not as Jack but as Dr. Donne, Dean of St. Paul's, and was famed for his preaching. The funerary effigy for which he posed dressed in his shroud is still to be seen, the only monument to survive the destruction of the old St. Paul's in the fire of 1666. Donne's last sermon was delivered there a month before he died, and according to Izaak Walton, his earliest biographer, many among those who "heard his faint and hollow voice" were conscious "that Dr. Donne *had preached his own funeral sermon.*" In it, as he lingered over "the *periods* and *transitions* in this life," he recalled his wife's own passage, fourteen years before: "In the wombe, the dead *child* kills the *Mother* that conceived it"; and later, "The *wombe* which should be the *house of life* becomes *death* it selfe, if *God* leave us there."

In thus implacably dwelling on mortal paradox, the writing of Donne is all of a piece—and of a piece as well with Hamlet's gravediggers and the *Urn Burial* of Sir Thomas Browne. Theirs was a time when outbreaks of plague were frequent, and when hitherto forbidden anatomical studies were soon to disclose the workings of the heart as an actual, physiological pump. From the beginning, Donne's poems are dense with allusions to the *"corruption* and *putrefaction* and *vermiculation* and *incineration,* and dispersion in and from the grave" that were to be the running theme of his sermons: not only carcasses and dissections, gout, fever, dropsy, powder burns, waking in a "cold quicksilver sweat," but colds and even fleabites. It has been said that the poetry of Donne is not sensuous—a strange commentary, it seems to me, on work so stunningly (and indeed at times revoltingly) physical. This quality was, I think, mainly why it interested me at a time when Wordsworth's didn't, or not very much. Even so patently formulaic and conventional a lyric as "The Bait," for me, leaped off the page and ran along the nerves:

> Let others freeze with angling reeds,
> And cut their legs, with shells and weeds,
> Or treacherously poor fish beset,
> With strangling snare, or windowy net:
>
> Let coarse bold hands, from slimy nest
> The bedded fish in banks out-wrest.

With all the brooding on mortality, and linked to it by some organic tissue, Donne had what Marianne Moore called gusto. He was interested in things. At his most self-centered—the accusation keeps being made, as though the self could be otherwise—he reaches out in all directions and to great distances: even on a voluptuous morning after, as he upbraids the sun for meddling, his imagination is global:

> Look, and tomorrow late, tell me
> Whether both th'Indias of spice and mine
> Be where thou left'st them, or lie here with me.

The original circumnavigation of the globe had been completed just half a century before Donne was born, and so vivid was his consciousness of it, of the fact that the world is round, contending as it did with the old geography, all those maps depicting the corners of the world, that the names of remote places seem to throng in wait, pressing for any mention however farfetched. In this Donne is like Emily Dickinson, who is sometimes linked with him on other grounds. Both speak of Tenerife, which neither had ever seen—though Donne himself traveled in its general direction when he sailed against Spain—but whose imagined altitude gave a value to the name itself. And so it becomes possible to connect the familiar lines from the second of the *Anniversaries*—

> Thou look'st through spectacles; small things seem great
> Below; but up unto the watch-tower get
> And see all things despoiled of fallacies

—with the cupola at Amherst, the seat of Emily Dickinson's uniquely incandescent vision of the world.

From his own watchtower, Donne had a vision otherwise quite different. All those voyages and discoveries notwithstanding, for him the world was *old*—was, as many seriously believed it to be, near the appointed end. Becalmed at Mitcham, Donne had written, as he did every Tuesday, to Sir Henry Goodyer—the closest of all his friends, and he had many—of the world out there as "a garment made of remnants, a life raveld out into ends, a line discontinued." That it gave him pleasure to think of the world in rags is, in the circumstances, hardly surprising. (He would caution himself presently against such ill-wishing.) At any rate, the notion of a thing in rags recurs through the poems: the rags of religion, in the third satire; the worn-out tufftaffaty worn by the purveyor of scandals at court, in the fourth; the rotting sails of "The Storm"; in "The Broken Heart," that organ itself as a thing of rags; and in "Good Friday, 1613. Riding Westward,"

> that flesh which was worn,
> By God, for his apparel, ragged, and torn?

The world in rags, as "but a carcase," as a ghost, as a dry cinder is the obsessive central theme of *The Anniversaries,* brought forth from the gloom and damp of Mitcham—whose two installments together constitute by far the longest (and in some ways the gloomiest) poem Donne ever wrote. It is—the more since it is a work Donne chose to publish, in 1611 and 1612—once again controversial. A masterpiece, or a maundering and outlandish occasional poem? Just possibly it is both. The occasion, as the title makes explicit, is "the untimely death of Mistress Elizabeth Drury"—a girl of fifteen, whom Donne may never have met, and to whose father, Sir Robert Drury, he hoped to recommend himself. Since "the frailty and decay of this whole world" are seen, for the purposes of the work at hand, to issue from her demise, there is a certain ricketyness about the project. Ben Jonson found it blasphemous. Marjorie Hope Nicolson thought it might be rescued if it were seen as a late-blooming elegy for another Elizabeth, the Virgin Queen who had died eight years before. It would be pleasing to think so—and almost possible, if Donne had not made what he was doing quite so explicit. He originally planned to go on producing an installment a year, as each new anniversary came round. But in 1612 (thanks to Sir Robert Drury, as it must be noted) his fortunes improved, he moved from Mitcham to London, and from then on there would have been less time anyhow. As it is, the poem runs on rather like an orator entangled in his own peroration. Readers of anthologies know it mainly by way of a purple patch or two. For this volume I have cut it by about half, hoping to disclose the unity without undercutting the reiterative force:

> She, she is dead; she's dead; when thou know'st this,
> Thou know'st how poor a trifling thing man is

through the culminating variant:

> She, she is gone; she is gone; when thou know'st this,
> What fragmentary rubbish this world is
> Thou know'st, and that it is not worth a thought.

All this is of course hyperbole, not literal assertion. What gives so unwieldy a production its surprising power is, I think, that Donne in fact cared a good deal about a world that is, after nearly four centuries, still so recognizable:

> 'Tis all in pieces, all coherence gone;
> All just supply, and all relation:
> Prince, subject, father, son, are things forgot,
> For every man alone thinks he hath got
> To be a phoenix, and that then can be
> None of that kind, of which he is, but he.

When Yeats wrote of how things fall apart, was he borrowing, even subconsciously? Or did he simply see the same thing happening all over again? In either event, not much in the poems of Donne is so likely to bring Yeats to mind. A more plausible inheritor would be Marianne Moore, for whom a paramount concern was with naturalness—with clearing away all the limp, pat, dreary, stilted locutions that inspired her dislike of Poetry with a capital *P*. The vivacity, the abrupt music, the occasional cacophony of the speaking voice: it is for these that the poems of Donne continue to be read. Eliot thought so—continued to think so even as he voiced his second thoughts: "It is hardly too much to say that Donne enlarged the possibilities of lyric verse as no other English poet has done."

This he did by making it newly dramatic. The cry of the girl in the elegy "On his Mistress"—"Oh, oh/ Nurse, O my love is slain, I saw him go/ O'er the white Alps alone"—has the ring of a speech from a play by Shakespeare. Donne was ventriloquist enough—or open enough, as I like to think—to have ventured more than one poem entirely in the voice of a woman: "Break of Day," "Confined Love," and the verse epistle "Sappho to Philaenis"—a piece Helen Gardner preferred to believe Donne could not have written, though John Carey allows it to stand, calling it "the first homosexual love poem in English"—are to be read so.

Elsewhere, the brisk syncopations of direct address roughen the surface of poems otherwise conventional. In "The Expiration," which I take to be early, the imperative becomes an enjambed leap from one stanza to the next:

> We asked none leave to love; nor will we owe
>   Any, so cheap a death, as saying, Go;
>
> Go . . .

More characteristic, and probably later (as I believe; but no one knows), is the way he can make anyone in the world his own interlocutor: "For God's sake, hold your tongue, and let me love."

More typical still is the speaker addressing his own soul: "What if this present were the world's last night?" This is the habitual mode of the sermons as well as of the religious lyrics:

> Who sees God's face, that is self life, must die;
> What a death were it then to see God die?
> It made his own lieutenant Nature shrink,
> It made his footstool crack, and the sun wink.
> Could I behold those hands which span the poles,
> And turn all spheres at once, pierced with those holes?

Lines such as these have an intensity the love poems nowhere quite equal. The extremes of a baroque sensibility are to be found throughout the works of Donne. But those extremes, the paradoxical hyperbole, here transcend their literary function to become a way of apprehending the stress of being—reality as a process, a condition to be entered rather than observed. Many readers, and I am one, have found it more confusing than helpful to refer to a metaphysical school of poets, the term having long ago become a catchall for whatever is merely ingenious, elaborate, or farfetched. But the greatest of Donne's religious poetry is metaphysical in the root sense of going beyond rational exploration. The "physics" of the early seventeenth century, with its persistent imagery of turning spheres, of macro- and microcosms, of hierarchy and degree, has been superseded. Yet the continuity of the human imagination is such that along with the speaking voice, the profane and sweaty ardor, the force of what John Donne most deeply believed is with us still.

The text of the poems that follow is from A. J. Smith's edition (Penguin Classics, 1986). Donne left no authorized texts other than those of *The Anniversaries,* published in 1611 and 1612, and his elegy for Prince Henry, published in 1613. There is accordingly much confusion and uncertainty about variant readings in the surviving manuscript copies, as well as about dating and sequence. Most editions follow that of one or another of the collections published after the poet's death. My own concern has been with finding a progression, both formal and thematic, from the more accessible works to those that for one reason or another seemed to make greater demands on the reader. A brief glossary has been appended; it is of course no substitute for the extensive annotation to be found in more comprehensive editions. As one who has frequently been thrilled by work she did not fully understand, I hope that from the selection offered here the essential Donne will emerge and speak to others as he has spoken to me.

—AMY CLAMPITT

Poems

I. SONGS, SATIRES, ELEGIES

The Expiration

So, so, break off this last lamenting kiss,
    Which sucks two souls, and vapours both away,
Turn thou ghost that way, and let me turn this,
    And let ourselves benight our happiest day,
We asked none leave to love; nor will we owe
    Any, so cheap a death, as saying, Go;

Go; and if that word have not quite killed thee,
    Ease me with death, by bidding me go too.
Oh, if it have, let my word work on me,
    And a just office on a murderer do.
Except it be too late, to kill me so,
    Being double dead, going, and bidding, go.

The Computation

For the first twenty years, since yesterday,
    I scarce believed, thou couldst be gone away,
For forty more, I fed on favours past,
    And forty on hopes, that thou wouldst, they might last.
Tears drowned one hundred, and sighs blew out two,

A thousand, I did neither think, nor do,
  Or not divide, all being one thought of you;
  Or in a thousand more, forgot that too.
Yet call not this long life; but think that I
Am, by being dead, immortal; can ghosts die?

The Bait

Come live with me, and be my love,
And we will some new pleasures prove
Of golden sands, and crystal brooks,
With silken lines, and silver hooks.

There will the river whispering run
Warmed by thy eyes, more than the sun.
And there the'enamoured fish will stay,
Begging themselves they may betray.

When thou wilt swim in that live bath,
Each fish, which every channel hath,
Will amorously to thee swim,
Gladder to catch thee, than thou him.

If thou, to be so seen, be'st loth,
By sun, or moon, thou darkenest both,
And if myself have leave to see,
I need not their light, having thee.

Let others freeze with angling reeds,
And cut their legs, with shells and weeds,
Or treacherously poor fish beset,
With strangling snare, or windowy net:

Let coarse bold hands, from slimy nest
The bedded fish in banks out-wrest,
Or curious traitors, sleavesilk flies
Bewitch poor fishes' wandering eyes.

For thee, thou need'st no such deceit,
For thou thyself art thine own bait,
That fish, that is not catched thereby,
Alas, is wiser far than I.

Song

Go, and catch a falling star,
   Get with child a mandrake root,
Tell me, where all past years are,
   Or who cleft the Devil's foot,
Teach me to hear mermaids singing,
   Or to keep off envy's stinging,
       And find
       What wind
Serves to advance an honest mind.

If thou be'est born to strange sights,
   Things invisible to see,
Ride ten thousand days and nights,
   Till age snow white hairs on thee,
Thou, when thou return'st, wilt tell me
All strange wonders that befell thee,
       And swear
       No where
Lives a woman true, and fair.

If thou find'st one, let me know,
 Such a pilgrimage were sweet,
Yet do not, I would not go,
 Though at next door we might meet,
Though she were true, when you met her,
And last, till you write your letter,
   Yet she
   Will be
False, ere I come, to two, or three.

Love's Deity

I long to talk with some old lover's ghost,
 Who died before the god of love was born:
I cannot think that he, who then loved most,
 Sunk so low, as to love one which did scorn.
But since this god produced a destiny,
And that vice-nature, custom, lets it be;
 I must love her, that loves not me.

Sure, they which made him god, meant not so much,
 Nor he, in his young godhead practised it.
But when an even flame two hearts did touch,
 His office was indulgently to fit
Actives to passives. Correspondency
Only his subject was; it cannot be
 Love, till I love her, that loves me.

But every modern god will now extend
 His vast prerogative, as far as Jove.
To rage, to lust, to write to, to commend,
 All is the purlieu of the god of love.
Oh were we wakened by this tyranny

To ungod this child again, it could not be
 I should love her, who loves not me.

Rebel and atheist too, why murmur I,
 As though I felt the worst that love could do?
Love might make me leave loving, or might try
 A deeper plague, to make her love me too,
Which, since she loves before, I am loth to see;
Falsehood is worse than hate; and that must be,
 If she whom I love, should love me.

Woman's Constancy

Now thou hast loved me one whole day,
Tomorrow when thou leav'st, what wilt thou say?
Wilt thou then antedate some new made vow?
   Or say that now
We are not just those persons, which we were?
Or, that oaths made in reverential fear
Of Love, and his wrath, any may forswear?
Or, as true deaths, true marriages untie,
So lovers' contracts, images of those,
Bind but till sleep, death's image, them unloose?
   Or, your own end to justify,
For having purposed change, and falsehood, you
Can have no way but falsehood to be true?
Vain lunatic, against these 'scapes I could
   Dispute, and conquer, if I would,
    Which I abstain to do,
For by tomorrow, I may think so too.

The Indifferent

I can love both fair and brown,
Her whom abundance melts, and her whom want betrays,
Her who loves loneness best, and her who masks and plays,
Her whom the country formed, and whom the town,
Her who believes, and her who tries,
Her who still weeps with spongy eyes,
And her who is dry cork, and never cries;
I can love her, and her, and you and you,
I can love any, so she be not true.

Will no other vice content you?
Will it not serve your turn to do, as did your mothers?
Have you old vices spent, and now would find out others?
Or doth a fear, that men are true, torment you?
Oh we are not, be not you so,
Let me, and do you, twenty know.
Rob me, but bind me not, and let me go.
Must I, who came to travail thorough you,
Grow your fixed subject, because you are true?

Venus heard me sigh this song,
And by love's sweetest part, variety, she swore,
She heard not this till now; and that it should be so no more.
She went, examined, and returned ere long,
And said, 'Alas, some two or three
Poor heretics in love there be,
Which think to establish dangerous constancy.
But I have told them, "Since you will be true,
You shall be true to them, who are false to you."'

Community

Good we must love, and must hate ill,
For ill is ill, and good good still,
   But there are things indifferent,
Which we may neither hate, nor love,
But one, and then another prove,
   As we shall find our fancy bent.

If then at first wise Nature had
Made women either good or bad,
   Then some we might hate, and some choose,
But since she did them so create,
That we may neither love, nor hate,
   Only this rests, All, all may use.

If they were good it would be seen,
Good is as visible as green,
   And to all eyes itself betrays:
If they were bad, they could not last,
Bad doth itself, and others waste,
   So, they deserve nor blame, nor praise.

But they are ours as fruits are ours,
He that but tastes, he that devours,
   And he that leaves all, doth as well:
Changed loves are but changed sorts of meat,
And when he hath the kernel eat,
   Who doth not fling away the shell?

The Flea

Mark but this flea, and mark in this,
How little that which thou deny'st me is;
Me it sucked first, and now sucks thee,
And in this flea, our two bloods mingled be;
Confess it, this cannot be said
A sin, or shame, or loss of maidenhead,
   Yet this enjoys before it woo,
    And pampered swells with one blood made of two,
    And this, alas, is more than we would do.

Oh stay, three lives in one flea spare,
Where we almost, nay more than married are.
This flea is you and I, and this
Our marriage bed, and marriage temple is;
Though parents grudge, and you, we'are met,
And cloistered in these living walls of jet.
   Though use make you apt to kill me,
    Let not to this, self murder added be,
    And sacrilege, three sins in killing three.

Cruel and sudden, hast thou since
Purpled thy nail, in blood of innocence?
In what could this flea guilty be,
Except in that drop which it sucked from thee?
Yet thou triumph'st, and say'st that thou
Find'st not thyself, nor me the weaker now;
   'Tis true, then learn how false, fears be;
    Just so much honour, when thou yield'st to me,
    Will waste, as this flea's death took life from thee.

The Curse

Whoever guesses, thinks, or dreams he knows
Who is my mistress, wither by this curse;
      His only, and only his purse
      May some dull heart to love dispose,
And she yield then to all that are his foes;
   May he be scorned by one, whom all else scorn,
   Forswear to others, what to her he hath sworn,
   With fear of missing, shame of getting, torn:

Madness his sorrow, gout his cramps, may he
Make, by but thinking, who hath made him such:
      And may he feel no touch
      Of conscience, but of fame, and be
Anguished not that 'twas sin, but that 'twas she:
   In early and long scarceness may he rot,
   For land which had been his, if he had not
   Himself incestuously an heir begot:

May he dream treason, and believe, that he
Meant to perform it, and confess, and die,
      And no record tell why:
      His sons, which none of his may be,
Inherit nothing but his infamy:
   Or may he so long parasites have fed,
   That he would fain be theirs, whom he hath bred,
   And at the last be circumcised for bread:

The venom of all stepdames, gamesters' gall,
What tyrants, and their subjects interwish,
      What plants, mines, beasts, fowl, fish,
      Can contribute, all ill which all
Prophets, or poets spake; and all which shall

Be annexed in schedules unto this by me,
Fall on that man; for if it be a she
Nature before hand hath out-cursed me.

The Message

Send home my long strayed eyes to me,
Which (oh) too long have dwelt on thee,
Yet since there they have learned such ill,
　　Such forced fashions,
　　And false passions,
　　　　That they be
　　　　Made by thee
Fit for no good sight, keep them still.

Send home my harmless heart again,
Which no unworthy thought could stain,
But if it be taught by thine
　　To make jestings
　　Of protestings,
　　　　And cross both
　　　　Word and oath,
Keep it, for then 'tis none of mine.

Yet send me back my heart and eyes,
That I may know, and see thy lies,
And may laugh and joy, when thou
　　Art in anguish
　　And dost languish
　　　　For some one
　　　　That will none,
Or prove as false as thou art now.

The Apparition

When by thy scorn, O murderess, I am dead,
And that thou think'st thee free
From all solicitation from me,
Then shall my ghost come to thy bed,
And thee, feigned vestal, in worse arms shall see;
Then thy sick taper will begin to wink,
And he, whose thou art then, being tired before,
Will, if thou stir, or pinch to wake him, think
    Thou call'st for more,
And in false sleep will from thee shrink,
And then poor aspen wretch, neglected thou
Bathed in a cold quicksilver sweat wilt lie
    A verier ghost than I;
What I will say, I will not tell thee now,
Lest that preserve thee; and since my love is spent,
I had rather thou shouldst painfully repent,
Than by my threatenings rest still innocent.

The Broken Heart

He is stark mad, who ever says,
    That he hath been in love an hour,
Yet not that love so soon decays,
    But that it can ten in less space devour;
Who will believe me, if I swear
That I have had the plague a year?
    Who would not laugh at me, if I should say,
    I saw a flask of powder burn a day?

Ah, what a trifle is a heart,
    If once into Love's hands it come!

All other griefs allow a part
    To other griefs, and ask themselves but some,
They come to us, but us Love draws,
He swallows us, and never chaws:
    By him, as by chain-shot, whole ranks do die,
    He is the tyrant pike, our hearts the fry.

If 'twere not so, what did become
    Of my heart, when I first saw thee?
I brought a heart into the room,
    But from the room, I carried none with me;
If it had gone to thee, I know
Mine would have taught thy heart to show
    More pity unto me: but Love, alas,
    At one first blow did shiver it as glass.

Yet nothing can to nothing fall,
    Nor any place be empty quite,
Therefore I think my breast hath all
    Those pieces still, though they be not unite;
And now as broken glasses show
A hundred lesser faces, so
    My rags of heart can like, wish, and adore,
    But after one such love, can love no more.

Break of Day

'Tis true, 'tis day, what though it be?
O wilt thou therefore rise from me?
Why should we rise, because 'tis light?
Did we lie down, because 'twas night?
Love which in spite of darkness brought us hither,
Should in despite of light keep us together.

Light hath no tongue, but is all eye;
If it could speak as well as spy,
This were the worst, that it could say,
That being well, I fain would stay,
And that I loved my heart and honour so,
That I would not from him, that had them, go.

Must business thee from hence remove?
Oh, that's the worst disease of love,
The poor, the foul, the false, love can
Admit but not the busied man.
He which hath business, and makes love, doth do
Such wrong, as when a married man doth woo.

Confined Love

Some man unworthy to be possessor
Of old or new love, himself being false or weak,
    Thought his pain and shame would be lesser,
If on womankind he might his anger wreak,
        And thence a law did grow,
        One should but one man know;
        But are other creatures so?

    Are sun, moon, or stars by law forbidden,
To smile where they list, or lend away their light?
    Are birds divorced, or are they chidden
If they leave their mate, or lie abroad a-night?
        Beasts do no jointures lose
        Though they new lovers choose,
        But we are made worse than those.

Who e'er rigged fair ship to lie in harbours
And not to seek new lands, or not to deal withal?
   Or built fair houses, set trees, and arbours,
Only to lock up, or else to let them fall?
      Good is not good, unless
      A thousand it possess,
      But doth waste with greediness.

From *Sappho to Philaenis*

. . . .
Thy body is a natural paradise,
   In whose self, unmanured, all pleasure lies,
Nor needs perfection; why shouldst thou then
   Admit the tillage of a harsh rough man?
Men leave behind them that which their sin shows,
   And are as thieves traced, which rob when it snows.
But of our dalliance no more signs there are,
   Than fishes leave in streams, or birds in air.
And between us all sweetness may be had;
   All, all that Nature yields, or Art can add.
My two lips, eyes, thighs, differ from thy two,
   But so, as thine from one another do;
And, oh, no more; the likeness being such,
   Why should they not alike in all parts touch?
Hand to strange hand, lip to lip none denies;
   Why should they breast to breast, or thighs to thighs?
Likeness begets such strange self flattery,
   That touching myself, all seems done to thee.
Myself I embrace, and mine own hands I kiss,
   And amorously thank myself for this.
Me, in my glass, I call thee; but alas,
   When I would kiss, tears dim mine eyes, and glass.

O cure this loving madness, and restore
   Me to me; thee, my half, my all, my more.
So may thy cheeks' red outwear scarlet dye,
   And their white, whiteness of the galaxy,
So may thy mighty, amazing beauty move
   Envy in all women, and in all men, love,
And so be change, and sickness, far from thee,
   As thou by coming near, keep'st them from me.

To his Mistress Going to Bed (Elegy 19)

Come, Madam, come, all rest my powers defy,
Until I labour, I in labour lie.
The foe oft-times having the foe in sight,
Is tired with standing though they never fight.
Off with that girdle, like heaven's zone glistering,
But a far fairer world encompassing.
Unpin that spangled breastplate which you wear,
That th' eyes of busy fools may be stopped there.
Unlace yourself, for that harmonious chime
Tells me from you, that now 'tis your bed time.
Off with that happy busk, which I envy,
That still can be, and still can stand so nigh.
Your gown going off, such beauteous state reveals,
As when from flowery meads th' hill's shadow steals.
Off with that wiry coronet and show
The hairy diadem which on you doth grow;
Now off with those shoes, and then safely tread
In this love's hallowed temple, this soft bed.
In such white robes heaven's angels used to be
Received by men; thou angel bring'st with thee
A heaven like Mahomet's paradise; and though
Ill spirits walk in white, we easily know

By this these angels from an evil sprite,
Those set our hairs, but these our flesh upright.
  Licence my roving hands, and let them go
Before, behind, between, above, below.
O my America, my new found land,
My kingdom, safeliest when with one man manned,
My mine of precious stones, my empery,
How blessed am I in this discovering thee!
To enter in these bonds, is to be free;
Then where my hand is set, my seal shall be.
  Full nakedness, all joys are due to thee.
As souls unbodied, bodies unclothed must be,
To taste whole joys. Gems which you women use
Are like Atlanta's balls, cast in men's views,
That when a fool's eye lighteth on a gem,
His earthly soul may covet theirs, not them.
Like pictures, or like books' gay coverings made
For laymen, are all women thus arrayed;
Themselves are mystic books, which only we
Whom their imputed grace will dignify
Must see revealed. Then since I may know,
As liberally, as to a midwife, show
Thyself: cast all, yea, this white linen hence,
Here is no penance, much less innocence.
  To teach thee, I am naked first, why then
What needst thou have more covering than a man.

The Good Morrow

I wonder by my troth, what thou, and I
    Did, till we loved? were we not weaned till then,
But sucked on country pleasures, childishly?
    Or snorted we in the seven sleepers' den?

'Twas so; but this, all pleasures fancies be.
If ever any beauty I did see,
Which I desired, and got, 'twas but a dream of thee.

And now good morrow to our waking souls,
Which watch not one another out of fear;
For love, all love of other sights controls,
And makes one little room, an every where.
Let sea-discoverers to new worlds have gone,
Let maps to others, worlds on worlds have shown,
Let us possess one world, each hath one, and is one.

My face in thine eye, thine in mine appears,
And true plain hearts do in the faces rest,
Where can we find two better hemispheres
Without sharp north, without declining west?
What ever dies, was not mixed equally;
If our two loves be one, or, thou and I
Love so alike, that none do slacken, none can die.

The Sun Rising

Busy old fool, unruly sun,
Why dost thou thus,
Through windows, and through curtains call on us?
Must to thy motions lovers' seasons run?
Saucy pedantic wretch, go chide
Late school-boys, and sour prentices,
Go tell court-huntsmen, that the King will ride,
Call country ants to harvest offices;
Love, all alike, no season knows, nor clime,
Nor hours, days, months, which are the rags of time.

Thy beams, so reverend, and strong
    Why shouldst thou think?
I could eclipse and cloud them with a wink,
But that I would not lose her sight so long:
    If her eyes have not blinded thine,
    Look, and tomorrow late, tell me,
    Whether both th'Indias of spice and mine
    Be where thou left'st them, or lie here with me.
Ask for those kings whom thou saw'st yesterday,
And thou shalt hear, All here in one bed lay.

    She'is all states, and all princes, I,
    Nothing else is.
Princes do but play us; compared to this,
All honour's mimic; all wealth alchemy.
    Thou sun art half as happy as we,
    In that the world's contracted thus;
    Thine age asks ease, and since thy duties be
    To warm the world, that's done in warming us.
Shine here to us, and thou art everywhere;
This bed thy centre is, these walls, thy sphere.

Jealousy (Elegy 1)

Fond woman, which wouldst have thy husband die,
And yet complain'st of his great jealousy;
If swoll'n with poison, he lay in his last bed,
His body with a sere-bark covered,
Drawing his breath, as thick and short, as can
The nimblest crocheting musician,
Ready with loathsome vomiting to spew
His soul out of one hell, into a new,
Made deaf with his poor kindred's howling cries,

Begging with few feigned tears, great legacies,
Thou wouldst not weep, but jolly, and frolic be,
As a slave, which tomorrow should be free;
Yet weep'st thou, when thou seest him hungerly
Swallow his own death, heart's-bane jealousy.
O give him many thanks, he is courteous,
That in suspecting kindly warneth us.
We must not, as we used, flout openly,
In scoffing riddles, his deformity;
Nor at his board together being sat,
With words, nor touch, scarce looks adulterate.
Nor when he swoll'n, and pampered with great fare,
Sits down, and snorts, caged in his basket chair,
Must we usurp his own bed any more,
Nor kiss and play in his house, as before.
Now I see many dangers; for that is
His realm, his castle, and his diocese.
But if, as envious men, which would revile
Their prince, or coin his gold, themselves exile
Into another country, and do it there,
We play in another house, what should we fear?
There we will scorn his household policies,
His silly plots, and pensionary spies,
As the inhabitants of Thames' right side
Do London's Mayor; or Germans, the Pope's pride.

Love's Exchange

Love, any devil else but you,
Would for a given soul give something too.
At Court your fellows every day,
Give th' art of rhyming, huntsmanship, and play,
For them who were their own before;

Only I have nothing which gave more,
But am, alas, by being lowly, lower.

I ask not dispensation now
To falsify a tear, or sigh, or vow,
   I do not sue from thee to draw
A *non obstante* on nature's law,
      These are prerogatives, they inhere
      In thee and thine; none should forswear
Except that he Love's minion were.

   Give me thy weakness, make me blind,
Both ways, as thou and thine, in eyes and mind;
   Love, let me never know that this
Is love, or, that love childish is.
      Let me not know that others know
      That she knows my pain, lest that so
A tender shame make me mine own new woe.

   If thou give nothing, yet thou'art just,
Because I would not thy first motions trust;
   Small towns which stand stiff, till great shot
Enforce them, by war's law condition not.
      Such in love's warfare is my case,
      I may not article for grace,
Having put Love at last to show this face.

   This face, by which he could command
And change the idolatry of any land,
   This face, which wheresoe'er it comes,
Can call vowed men from cloisters, dead from tombs,
      And melt both poles at once, and store
      Deserts with cities, and make more
Mines in the earth, than quarries were before.

For this Love is enraged with me,
Yet kills not. If I must example be
To future rebels; if th' unborn
Must learn, by my being cut up, and torn:
Kill, and dissect me, Love; for this
Torture against thine own end is,
Racked carcases make ill anatomies.

The Will

Before I sigh my last gasp, let me breathe,
Great Love, some legacies; here I bequeath
Mine eyes to Argus, if mine eyes can see,
If they be blind, then Love, I give them thee;
My tongue to fame; to ambassadors mine ears;
To women or the sea, my tears.
Thou, Love, hast taught me heretofore
By making me serve her who had twenty more,
That I should give to none, but such, as had too much before.

My constancy I to the planets give;
My truth to them, who at the Court do live;
Mine ingenuity and openness,
To Jesuits; to buffoons my pensiveness;
My silence to any, who abroad hath been;
My money to a Capuchin.
Thou Love taught'st me, by appointing me
To love there, where no love received can be,
Only to give to such as have an incapacity.

My faith I give to Roman Catholics;
All my good works unto the schismatics
Of Amsterdam; my best civility

And courtship, to an university;
My modesty I give to soldiers bare;
    My patience let gamesters share.
Thou Love taught'st me, by making me
Love her that holds my love disparity,
Only to give to those that count my gifts indignity.

I give my reputation to those
Which were my friends; mine industry to foes;
To schoolmen I bequeath my doubtfulness;
My sickness to physicians, or excess;
To Nature, all that I in rhyme have writ;
    And to my company my wit.
Thou Love, by making me adore
Her, who begot this love in me before,
Taught'st me to make, as though I gave, when I did but
    restore.

To him for whom the passing bell next tolls,
I give my physic books; my written rolls
Of moral counsels, I to Bedlam give;
My brazen medals, unto them which live
In want of bread; to them which pass among
    All foreigners, mine English tongue.
Thou, Love, by making me love one
Who thinks her friendship a fit portion
For younger lovers, dost my gifts thus disproportion.

Therefore I'll give no more; but I'll undo
The world by dying; because love dies too.
Then all your beauties will be no more worth
Than gold in mines, where none doth draw it forth;
And all your graces no more use shall have
    Than a sundial in a grave.

Thou Love taught'st me, by making me
Love her, who doth neglect both me and thee,
To invent, and practise this one way, to annihilate all three.

Satire 2

Sir; though (I thank God for it) I do hate
Perfectly all this town, yet there's one state
In all ill things so excellently best,
That hate, towards them, breeds pity towards the rest.
Though poetry indeed be such a sin
As I think that brings dearths, and Spaniards in,
Though like the pestilence and old fashioned love,
Riddlingly it catch men; and doth remove
Never, till it be starved out; yet their state
Is poor, disarmed, like papists, not worth hate.
One (like a wretch, which at Bar judged as dead,
Yet prompts him which stands next, and cannot read,
And saves his life) gives idiot actors means
(Starving himself) to live by his laboured scenes;
As in some organ, puppets dance above
And bellows pant below, which them do move.
One would move love by rhymes; but witchcraft's charms
Bring not now their old fears, nor their old harms:
Rams, and slings now are silly battery,
Pistolets are the best artillery.
And they who write to lords, rewards to get,
Are they not like singers at doors for meat?
And they who write, because all write, have still
That excuse for writing, and for writing ill.
But he is worst, who (beggarly) doth chaw
Others' wits' fruits, and in his ravenous maw
Rankly digested, doth those things out spew,

As his own things; and they are his own, 'tis true,
For if one eat my meat, though it be known
The meat was mine, th' excrement is his own.
But these do me no harm, nor they which use
To outdo dildoes, and out-usure Jews;
To out-drink the sea, to outswear the Litany;
Who with sins' all kinds as familiar be
As confessors; and for whose sinful sake,
Schoolmen new tenements in hell must make:
Whose strange sins, canonists could hardly tell
In which commandment's large receipt they dwell.
    But these punish themselves; the insolence
Of Coscus only breeds my just offence,
Whom time (which rots all, and makes botches pox,
And plodding on, must make a calf an ox)
Hath made a lawyer, which was alas of late
But a scarce poet; jollier of this state,
Than are new beneficed ministers, he throws
Like nets, or lime-twigs, wheresoe'er he goes,
His title of barrister, on every wench,
And woos in language of the Pleas, and Bench:
'A motion, Lady'; 'Speak Coscus'; 'I have been
In love, ever since *tricesimo* of the Queen,
Continual claims I have made, injunctions got
To stay my rival's suit, that he should not
Proceed'; 'Spare me'; 'In Hilary term I went,
You said, if I returned next 'size in Lent,
I should be in remitter of your grace;
In th' interim my letters should take place
Of affidavits'; words, words, which would tear
The tender labyrinth of a soft maid's ear,
More, more, than ten Sclavonians scolding, more
Than when winds in our ruined abbeys roar.
When sick with poetry, and possessed with Muse

Thou wast, and mad, I hoped; but men which choose
Law practice for mere gain, bold soul, repute
Worse than embrothelled strumpets prostitute.
Now like an owl-like watchman, he must walk
His hand still at a bill, now he must talk
Idly, like prisoners, which whole months will swear
That only suretyship hath brought them there,
And to every suitor lie in everything,
Like a king's favourite, yea like a king;
Like a wedge in a block, wring to the bar,
Bearing like asses, and more shameless far
Than carted whores, lie, to the grave judge; for
Bastardy abounds not in kings' titles, nor
Simony and sodomy in churchmen's lives,
As these things do in him; by these he thrives.
Shortly (as the sea) he will compass all our land;
From Scots, to Wight; from Mount, to Dover strand.
And spying heirs melting with luxury,
Satan will not joy at their sins, as he.
For as a thrifty wench scrapes kitchen stuff,
And barrelling the droppings, and the snuff,
Of wasting candles, which in thirty year
(Relic-like kept) perchance buys wedding gear;
Piecemeal he gets lands, and spends as much time
Wringing each acre, as men pulling prime.
In parchments then, large as his fields, he draws
Assurances, big, as glossed civil laws,
So huge, that men (in our time's forwardness)
Are Fathers of the Church for writing less.
These he writes not; nor for these written pays,
Therefore spares no length; as in those first days
When Luther was professed, he did desire
Short *Pater nosters,* saying as a friar
Each day his beads, but having left those laws,

Adds to Christ's prayer, the power and glory clause.
But when he sells or changes land, he impairs
His writings, and (unwatched) leaves out, *ses heires,*
As slily as any commenter goes by
Hard words, or sense; or in Divinity
As controverters, in vouched texts, leave out
Shrewd words, which might against them clear the doubt.
Where are those spread woods which clothed heretofore
Those bought lands? not built, nor burnt within door.
Where's th' old landlord's troops, and alms? In great halls
Carthusian fasts, and fulsome bacchanals
Equally I hate; means bless; in rich men's homes
I bid kill some beasts, but no hecatombs,
None starve, none surfeit so; but oh we allow,
Good works as good, but out of fashion now,
Like old rich wardrobes; but my words none draws
Within the vast reach of the huge statute laws.

Satire 3

Kind pity chokes my spleen; brave scorn forbids
Those tears to issue which swell my eye-lids,
I must not laugh, nor weep sins, and be wise,
Can railing then cure these worn maladies?
Is not our mistress fair religion,
As worthy of all our soul's devotion,
As virtue was to the first blinded age?
Are not heaven's joys as valiant to assuage
Lusts, as earth's honour was to them? Alas,
As we do them in means, shall they surpass
Us in the end, and shall thy father's spirit
Meet blind philosophers in heaven, whose merit
Of strict life may be imputed faith, and hear

Thee, whom he taught so easy ways and near
To follow, damned? O if thou dar'st, fear this;
This fear great courage, and high valour is.
Dar'st thou aid mutinous Dutch, and dar'st thou lay
Thee in ships' wooden sepulchres, a prey
To leaders' rage, to storms, to shot, to dearth?
Dar'st thou dive seas, and dungeons of the earth?
Hast thou courageous fire to thaw the ice
Of frozen north discoveries? and thrice
Colder than salamanders, like divine
Children in th'oven, fires of Spain, and the line,
Whose countries limbecks to our bodies be,
Canst thou for gain bear? and must every he
Which cries not, 'Goddess!' to thy mistress, draw,
Or eat thy poisonous words? courage of straw!
O desperate coward, wilt thou seem bold, and
To thy foes and his (who made thee to stand
Sentinel in his world's garrison) thus yield,
And for forbidden wars, leave th'appointed field?
Know thy foes: the foul Devil, he, whom thou
Strivest to please, for hate, not love, would allow
Thee fain, his whole realm to be quit; and as
The world's all parts wither away and pass,
So the world's self, thy other loved foe, is
In her decrepit wane, and thou loving this,
Dost love a withered and worn strumpet; last,
Flesh (itself's death) and joys which flesh can taste,
Thou lovest; and thy fair goodly soul, which doth
Give this flesh power to taste joy, thou dost loathe.
    Seek true religion. O where? Mirreus
Thinking her unhoused here, and fled from us,
Seeks her at Rome, there, because he doth know
That she was there a thousand years ago,
He loves her rags so, as we here obey

The statecloth where the Prince sate yesterday.
Grants to such brave loves will not be enthralled,
But loves her only, who at Geneva is called
Religion, plain, simple, sullen, young,
Contemptuous, yet unhandsome; as among
Lecherous humours, there is one that judges
No wenches wholesome, but coarse country drudges.
Graius stays still at home here, and because
Some preachers, vile ambitious bawds, and laws
Still new like fashions, bid him think that she
Which dwells with us, is only perfect, he
Embraceth her, whom his godfathers will
Tender to him, being tender, as wards still
Take such wives as their guardians offer, or
Pay values. Careless Phrygius doth abhor
All, because all cannot be good, as one
Knowing some women whores, dares marry none.
Gracchus loves all as one, and thinks that so
As women do in divers countries go
In divers habits, yet are still one kind,
So doth, so is religion; and this blind-
ness too much light breeds; but unmoved thou
Of force must one, and forced but one allow;
And the right; ask thy father which is she,
Let him ask his; though truth and falsehood be
Near twins, yet truth a little elder is;
Be busy to seek her, believe me this,
He's not of none, nor worst, that seeks the best.
To adore, or scorn an image, or protest,
May all be bad; doubt wisely, in strange way
To stand inquiring right, is not to stray;
To sleep, or run wrong is. On a huge hill,
Cragged, and steep, Truth stands, and he that will
Reach her, about must, and about must go;

And what the hill's suddenness resists, win so;
Yet strive so, that before age, death's twilight,
Thy soul rest, for none can work in that night,
To will, implies delay, therefore now do.
Hard deeds, the body's pains; hard knowledge too
The mind's endeavours reach, and mysteries
Are like the sun, dazzling, yet plain to all eyes.
Keep the truth which thou hast found; men do not stand
In so ill case here, that God hath with his hand
Signed kings blank-charters to kill whom they hate,
Nor are they vicars, but hangmen to Fate.
Fool and wretch, wilt thou let thy soul be tied
To man's laws, by which she shall not be tried
At the last day? Or will it then boot thee
To say a Philip, or a Gregory,
A Harry, or a Martin taught thee this?
Is not this excuse for mere contraries,
Equally strong; cannot both sides say so?
That thou mayest rightly obey power, her bounds know;
Those past, her nature, and name is changed; to be
Then humble to her is idolatry.
As streams are, power is; those blessed flowers that dwell
At the rough stream's calm head, thrive and prove well,
But having left their roots, and themselves given
To the stream's tyrannous rage, alas are driven
Through mills, and rocks, and woods, and at last, almost
Consumed in going, in the sea are lost:
So perish souls, which more choose men's unjust
Power from God claimed, than God himself to trust.

Satire 4

Well; I may now receive, and die; my sin
Indeed is great, but I have been in
A purgatory, such as feared hell is
A recreation, and scant map of this.
My mind, neither with pride's itch, nor yet hath been
Poisoned with love to see, or to be seen.
I had no suit there, nor new suit to show,
Yet went to Court; but as Glaze which did go
To a Mass in jest, catched, was fain to disburse
The hundred marks, which is the Statute's curse,
Before he 'scaped, so it pleased my destiny
(Guilty of my sin of going), to think me
As prone to all ill, and of good as forget-
ful, as proud, as lustful, and as much in debt,
As vain, as witless, and as false as they
Which dwell at Court, for once going that way.
Therefore I suffered this; towards me did run
A thing more strange than on Nile's slime the sun
E'er bred, or all which into Noah's Ark came:
A thing, which would have posed Adam to name:
Stranger than seven antiquaries' studies,
Than Afric's monsters, Guiana's rarities,
Stranger than strangers; one, who for a Dane,
In the Danes' Massacre had sure been slain,
If he had lived then; and without help dies,
When next the 'prentices 'gainst strangers rise.
One, whom the watch at noon lets scarce go by,
One, to whom, the examining Justice sure would cry,
'Sir, by your priesthood tell me what you are.'
His clothes were strange, though coarse; and black, though bare;
Sleeveless his jerkin was, and it had been
Velvet, but 'twas now (so much ground was seen)

Become tufftaffaty; and our children shall
See it plain rash awhile, then naught at all.
This thing hath travelled, and saith, speaks all tongues
And only knoweth what to all states belongs,
Made of th' accents, and best phrase of all these,
He speaks one language; if strange meats displease,
Art can deceive, or hunger force my taste,
But pedant's motley tongue, soldier's bombast,
Mountebank's drugtongue, nor the terms of law
Are strong enough preparatives, to draw
Me to bear this, yet I must be content
With his tongue: in his tongue, called compliment:
In which he can win widows, and pay scores,
Make men speak treason, cozen subtlest whores,
Out-flatter favourites, or out-lie either
Jovius, or Surius, or both together.
He names me, and comes to me; I whisper, 'God!
How have I sinned, that thy wrath's furious rod,
This fellow, chooseth me?' He sayeth, 'Sir,
I love your judgement; whom do you prefer,
For the best linguist?' And I sillily
Said, that I thought Calepine's Dictionary;
'Nay but of men, most sweet Sir'. Beza then,
Some Jesuits, and two reverend men
Of our two Academies, I named. There
He stopped me, and said; 'Nay, your Apostles were
Good pretty linguists, and so Panurge was;
Yet a poor gentleman, all these may pass
By travail.' Then, as if he would have sold
His tongue, he praised it, and such wonders told
That I was fain to say, 'If you had lived, Sir,
Time enough to have been interpreter
To Babel's bricklayers, sure the Tower had stood.'
He adds, 'If of Court life you knew the good,

You would leave loneness.' I said, 'Not alone
My loneness is; but Spartan's fashion,
To teach by painting drunkards, doth not last
Now; Aretine's pictures have made few chaste;
No more can princes' Courts, though there be few
Better pictures of vice, teach me virtue';
He, like to a high stretched lute string squeaked, 'O Sir,
'Tis sweet to talk of kings.' 'At Westminster,'
Said I, 'the man that keeps the Abbey tombs,
And for his price doth with whoever comes,
Of all our Harrys, and our Edwards talk,
From king to king and all their kin can walk:
Your ears shall hear naught, but kings; your eyes meet
Kings only; The way to it, is King Street.'
He smacked, and cried, 'He's base, mechanic, coarse,
So are all your Englishmen in their discourse.
Are not your Frenchmen neat?' 'Mine? as you see,
I have but one Frenchman, look, he follows me.'
'Certes they are neatly clothed. I of this mind am,
Your only wearing is your grogaram.'
'Not so Sir, I have more.' Under this pitch
He would not fly; I chaffed him; but as itch
Scratched into smart, and as blunt iron ground
Into an edge, hurts worse: so, I (fool) found,
Crossing hurt me; to fit my sullenness,
He to another key his style doth dress,
And asks, 'What news?' I tell him of new plays.
He takes my hand, and as a still, which stays
A semi-breve 'twixt each drop, he niggardly,
As loth to enrich me, so tells many a lie,
More than ten Holinsheds, or Halls, or Stows,
Of trivial household trash he knows; he knows
When the Queen frowned, or smiled, and he knows what
A subtle statesman may gather of that;

He knows who loves; whom; and who by poison
Hastes to an office's reversion;
He knows who hath sold his land, and now doth beg
A license, old iron, boots, shoes, and egg-
Shells to transport; shortly boys shall not play
At span-counter, or blow-point, but they pay
Toll to some courtier; and wiser than all us,
He knows what lady is not painted; thus
He with home-meats tries me; I belch, spew, spit,
Look pale, and sickly, like a patient; yet
He thrusts on more; and as if he undertook
To say *Gallo-Belgicus* without book
Speaks of all states, and deeds, that have been since
The Spaniards came, to the loss of Amiens.
Like a big wife, at sight of loathed meat,
Ready to travail: so I sigh, and sweat
To hear this Macaron talk: in vain; for yet,
Either my humour, or his own to fit,
He like a privileged spy, whom nothing can
Discredit, libels now 'gainst each great man.
He names a price for every office paid;
He saith, our wars thrive ill, because delayed;
That offices are entailed, and that there are
Perpetuities of them, lasting as far
As the last day; and that great officers,
Do with the pirates share, and Dunkirkers.
Who wastes in meat, in clothes, in horse, he notes;
Who loves whores, who boys, and who goats.
I more amazed than Circe's prisoners, when
They felt themselves turn beasts, felt myself then
Becoming traitor, and methought I saw
One of our giant Statutes ope his jaw
To suck me in; for hearing him, I found
That as burnt venomed lechers do grow sound

By giving others their sores, I might grow
Guilty, and he free: therefore I did show
All signs of loathing; but since I am in,
I must pay mine, and my forefathers' sin
To the last farthing; therefore to my power
Toughly and stubbornly I bear this cross; but the hour
Of mercy now was come; he tries to bring
Me to pay a fine to 'scape his torturing,
And says, 'Sir, can you spare me'; I said, 'Willingly';
'Nay, Sir, can you spare me a crown?' Thankfully I
Gave it, as ransom; but as fiddlers, still,
Though they be paid to be gone, yet needs will
Thrust one more jig upon you; so did he
With his long complimental thanks vex me.
But he is gone, thanks to his needy want,
And the prerogative of my crown: scant
His thanks were ended, when I, (which did see
All the Court filled with more strange things than he)
Ran from thence with such or more haste, than one
Who fears more actions, doth make from prison.
    At home in wholesome solitariness
My precious soul began, the wretchedness
Of suitors at Court to mourn, and a trance
Like his, who dreamed he saw hell, did advance
Itself on me, such men as he saw there,
I saw at Court, and worse, and more; low fear
Becomes the guilty, not the accuser; then,
Shall I, none's slave, of high-born, or raised men
Fear frowns? And, my mistress Truth, betray thee
To th' huffing braggart, puffed nobility?
No, no, thou which since yesterday hast been
Almost about the whole world, hast thou seen,
O sun, in all thy journey, vanity,
Such as swells the bladder of our Court? I

Think he which made your waxen garden, and
Transported it from Italy to stand
With us, at London, flouts our Presence, for
Just such gay painted things, which no sap, nor
Taste have in them, ours are; and natural
Some of the stocks are, their fruits, bastard all.
        'Tis ten a-clock and past; all whom the mews,
Balloon, tennis, diet, or the stews,
Had all the morning held, now the second
Time made ready, that day, in flocks, are found
In the Presence, and I, (God pardon me).
As fresh, and sweet their apparels be, as be
The fields they sold to buy them; 'For a King
Those hose are,' cry the flatterers; and bring
Them next week to the theatre to sell;
Wants reach all states; me seems they do as well
At stage, as Court; all are players; whoe'er looks
(For themselves dare not go) o'er Cheapside books,
Shall find their wardrobe's inventory. Now,
The ladies come; as pirates, which do know
That there came weak ships fraught with cochineal,
The men board them; and praise, as they think, well,
Their beauties; they the men's wits; both are bought.
Why good wits ne'er wear scarlet gowns, I thought
This cause: these men, men's wits for speeches buy,
And women buy all reds which scarlets dye.
He called her beauty lime-twigs, her hair net;
She fears her drugs ill laid, her hair loose set.
Would not Heraclitus laugh to see Macrine,
From hat, to shoe, himself at door refine,
As if the Presence were a moschite, and lift
His skirts and hose, and call his clothes to shrift,
Making them confess not only mortal
Great stains and holes in them, but venial

Feathers and dust, wherewith they fornicate;
And then by Dürer's rules survey the state
Of his each limb, and with strings the odds tries
Of his neck to his leg, and waist to thighs.
So in immaculate clothes, and symmetry
Perfect as circles, with such nicety
As a young preacher at his first time goes
To preach, he enters, and a lady which owes
Him not so much as good will, he arrests,
And unto her protests protests protests
So much as at Rome would serve to have thrown
Ten Cardinals into the Inquisition;
And whispered 'By Jesu', so often, that a
Pursuivant would have ravished him away
For saying of our Lady's psalter; but 'tis fit
That they each other plague, they merit it.
But here comes Glorius that will plague them both,
Who, in the other extreme, only doth
Call a rough carelessness, good fashion;
Whose cloak his spurs tear; whom he spits on
He cares not, his ill words do no harm
To him; he rusheth in, as if 'Arm, arm,'
He meant to cry; and though his face be as ill
As theirs which in old hangings whip Christ, still
He strives to look worse, he keeps all in awe;
Jests like a licensed fool, commands like law.

Tired, now I leave this place, and but pleased so
As men which from gaols to execution go,
Go through the great chamber (why is it hung
With the seven deadly sins?). Being among
Those Ascaparts, men big enough to throw
Charing Cross for a bar, men that do know
No token of worth, but Queen's man, and fine
Living, barrels of beef, flagons of wine,

I shook like a spied spy. Preachers which are
Seas of wit and arts, you can, then dare,
Drown the sins of this place, for, for me
Which am but a scarce brook, it enough shall be
To wash the stains away; though I yet
With Maccabees' modesty, the known merit
Of my work lessen: yet some wise man shall,
I hope, esteem my writs canonical.

Satire 5

Thou shalt not laugh in this leaf, Muse, nor they
Whom any pity warms; he which did lay
Rules to make courtiers, (he being understood
May make good courtiers, but who courtiers good?)
Frees from the sting of jests all who in extreme
Are wretched or wicked: of these two a theme
Charity and liberty give me. What is he
Who officers' rage, and suitors' misery
Can write, and jest? If all things be in all,
As I think, since all, which were, are, and shall
Be, be made of the same elements:
Each thing, each thing implies or represents.
Then man is a world; in which, officers
Are the vast ravishing seas; and suitors,
Springs; now full, now shallow, now dry; which, to
That which drowns them, run: these self reasons do
Prove the world a man, in which, officers
Are the devouring stomach, and suitors
The excrements, which they void. All men are dust,
How much worse are suitors, who to men's lust
Are made preys. O worse than dust, or worm's meat,
For they do eat you now, whose selves worms shall eat.

They are the mills which grind you, yet you are
The wind which drives them; and a wasteful war
Is fought against you, and you fight it; they
Adulterate law, and you prepare their way
Like wittols; th' issue your own ruin is.
    Greatest and fairest Empress, know you this?
Alas, no more than Thames' calm head doth know
Whose meads her arms drown, or whose corn o'erflow:
You Sir, whose righteousness she loves, whom I
By having leave to serve, am most richly
For service paid, authorized, now begin
To know and weed out this enormous sin.
    O age of rusty iron! Some better wit
Call it some worse name, if aught equal it;
The Iron Age that was, when justice was sold, now
Injustice is sold dearer far; allow
All demands, fees, and duties; gamesters, anon
The money which you sweat, and swear for, is gone
Into other hands: so controverted lands
'Scape, like Angelica, the strivers' hands.
If law be in the judge's heart, and he
Have no heart to resist letter, or fee,
Where wilt thou appeal? power of the courts below
Flow from the first main head, and these can throw
Thee, if they suck thee in, to misery,
To fetters, halters; but if the injury
Steel thee to dare complain, alas, thou go'st
Against the stream, when upwards: when thou art most
Heavy and most faint; and in these labours they,
'Gainst whom thou shouldst complain, will in the way
Become great seas, o'er which, when thou shalt be
Forced to make golden bridges, thou shalt see
That all thy gold was drowned in them before;
All things follow their like, only who have may have more.
Judges are gods; he who made and said them so,

Meant not that men should be forced to them to go,
By means of angels; when supplications
We send to God, to Dominations,
Powers, Cherubins, and all heaven's courts, if we
Should pay fees as here, daily bread would be
Scarce to kings; so 'tis. Would it not anger
A stoic, a coward, yea a martyr,
To see a pursuivant come in, and call
All his clothes, copes; books, primers; and all
His plate, chalices; and mistake them away,
And ask a fee for coming? Oh, ne'er may
Fair Law's white reverend name be strumpeted,
To warrant thefts: she is established
Recorder to Destiny, on earth, and she
Speaks Fate's words, and but tells us who must be
Rich, who poor, who in chairs, who in gaols:
She is all fair, but yet hath foul long nails,
With which she scratcheth suitors; in bodies
Of men, so in law, nails are th' extremities,
So officers stretch to more than Law can do,
As our nails reach what no else part comes to.
Why barest thou to yon officer? Fool, hath he
Got those goods, for which erst men bared to thee?
Fool, twice, thrice, thou hast bought wrong, and now hungerly
Begg'st right; but that dole comes not till these die.
Thou hadst much, and law's Urim and Thummim try
Thou wouldst for more; and for all hast paper
Enough to clothe all the Great Carrack's pepper.
Sell that, and by that thou much more shalt leese,
Than Haman, when he sold his antiquities.
O wretch that thy fortunes should moralize
Aesop's fables, and make tales, prophecies.
Thou'rt the swimming dog whom shadows cozened,
And div'st, near drowning, for what vanished.

From *Metempsychosis*

31

Into an embryon fish, our soul is thrown,
And in due time thrown out again, and grown
To such vastness as, if unmanacled
From Greece, Morea were, and that by some
Earthquake unrooted, loose Morea swum,
Or seas from Afric's body had severed
And torn the hopeful promontory's head,
This fish would seem these, and, when all hopes fail,
A great ship overset, or without sail
    Hulling, might (when this was a whelp) be like this
      whale.

32

At every stroke his brazen fins do take,
More circles in the broken sea they make
Than cannons' voices, when the air they tear:
His ribs are pillars, and his high arched roof
Of bark that blunts best steel, is thunder-proof:
Swim in him swallowed dolphins, without fear,
And feel no sides, as if his vast womb were
Some inland sea, and ever as he went
He spouted rivers up, as if he meant
    To join our seas, with seas above the firmament.

33

He hunts not fish, but as an officer,
Stays in his court, as his own net, and there
All suitors of all sorts themselves enthral;
So on his back lies this whale wantoning,
And in his gulf-like throat, sucks every thing

That passeth near. Fish chaseth fish, and all,
Flyer and follower, in this whirlpool fall;
O might not states of more equality
Consist? and is it of necessity
 That thousand guiltless smalls, to make one great, must
  die?

34

Now drinks he up seas, and he eats up flocks,
He jostles islands, and he shakes firm rocks.
Now in a roomful house this soul doth float,
And like a Prince she sends her faculties
To all her limbs, distant as provinces.
The sun hath twenty times both crab and goat
Parched, since first launched forth this living boat.
'Tis greatest now, and to destruction
Nearest; there's no pause at perfection.
 Greatness a period hath, but hath no station.

The Storm

TO MR CHRISTOPHER BROOKE

Thou which art I, ('tis nothing to be so)
Thou which art still thyself, by these shalt know
Part of our passage; and, a hand, or eye
By Hilliard drawn, is worth an history,
By a worse painter made; and (without pride)
When by thy judgement they are dignified,
My lines are such: 'tis the pre-eminence
Of friendship only to impute excellence.
England to whom we owe, what we be, and have,
Sad that her sons did seek a foreign grave

(For, Fate's, or Fortune's drifts none can soothsay,
Honour and misery have one face and way)
From out her pregnant entrails sighed a wind
Which at th' air's middle marble room did find
Such strong resistance, that itself it threw
Downward again; and so when it did view
How in the port, our fleet dear time did leese,
Withering like prisoners, which lie but for fees,
Mildly it kissed our sails, and, fresh and sweet,
As to a stomach starved, whose insides meet,
Meat comes, it came; and swole our sails, when we
So joyed, as Sara her swelling joyed to see.
But 'twas but so kind, as our countrymen,
Which bring friends one day's way, and leave them then.
Then like two mighty kings, which dwelling far
Asunder, meet against a third to war,
The south and west winds joined, and, as they blew,
Waves like a rolling trench before them threw.
Sooner than you read this line, did the gale,
Like shot, not feared till felt, our sails assail;
And what at first was called a gust, the same
Hath now a storm's, anon a tempest's name.
Jonas, I pity thee, and curse those men,
Who when the storm raged most, did wake thee then;
Sleep is pain's easiest salve, and doth fulfil
All offices of death, except to kill.
But when I waked, I saw, that I saw not.
I, and the sun, which should teach me had forgot
East, west, day, night, and I could only say,
If the world had lasted, now it had been day.
Thousands our noises were, yet we 'mongst all
Could none by his right name, but thunder call:
Lightning was all our light, and it rained more
Than if the sun had drunk the sea before.

Some coffined in their cabins lie, equally
Grieved that they are not dead, and yet must die.
And as sin-burdened souls from graves will creep,
At the last day, some forth their cabins peep:
And tremblingly ask what news, and do hear so,
Like jealous husbands, what they would not know.
Some sitting on the hatches, would seem there,
With hideous gazing to fear away fear.
Then note they the ship's sicknesses, the mast
Shaked with this ague, and the hold and waist
With a salt dropsy clogged, and all our tacklings
Snapping, like too high stretched treble strings.
And from our tottered sails, rags drop down so,
As from one hanged in chains, a year ago.
Even our ordnance placed for our defence,
Strive to break loose, and 'scape away from thence.
Pumping hath tired our men, and what's the gain?
Seas into seas thrown, we suck in again;
Hearing hath deafed our sailors; and if they
Knew how to hear, there's none knows what to say.
Compared to these storms, death is but a qualm,
Hell somewhat lightsome, and the Bermuda calm.
Darkness, light's elder brother, his birth-right
Claims o'er this world, and to heaven hath chased light.
All things are one, and that one none can be,
Since all forms, uniform deformity
Doth cover, so that we, except God say
Another *Fiat,* shall have no more day.
So violent, yet long these furies be,
That though thine absence starve me, I wish not thee.

The Calm

Our storm is past, and that storm's tyrannous rage,
A stupid calm, but nothing it, doth 'suage.
The fable is inverted, and far more
A block afflicts, now, than a stork before.
Storms chafe, and soon wear out themselves, or us;
In calms, heaven laughs to see us languish thus.
As steady as I can wish, that my thoughts were,
Smooth as thy mistress' glass, or what shines there,
The sea is now. And, as those Isles which we
Seek, when we can move, our ships rooted be.
As water did in storms, now pitch runs out
As lead, when a fired church becomes one spout.
And all our beauty, and our trim, decays,
Like courts removing, or like ended plays.
The fighting place now seamen's rags supply;
And all the tackling is a frippery.
No use of lanthorns; and in one place lay
Feathers and dust, today and yesterday.
Earth's hollownesses, which the world's lungs are,
Have no more wind than the upper vault of air.
We can nor lost friends, nor sought foes recover,
But meteor-like, save that we move not, hover.
Only the calenture together draws
Dear friends, which meet dead in great fishes' jaws:
And on the hatches as on altars lies
Each one, his own priest, and own sacrifice.
Who live, that miracle do multiply
Where walkers in hot ovens, do not die.
If in despite of these, we swim, that hath
No more refreshing, than our brimstone bath,
But from the sea, into the ship we turn,
Like parboiled wretches, on the coals to burn.

Like Bajazet encaged, the shepherd's scoff,
Or like slack-sinewed Samson, his hair off,
Languish our ships. Now, as a myriad
Of ants, durst th' Emperor's loved snake invade,
The crawling galleys, sea-gaols, finny chips,
Might brave our pinnaces, now bed-rid ships.
Whether a rotten state, and hope of gain,
Or, to disuse me from the queasy pain
Of being beloved, and loving, or the thirst
Of honour, or fair death, out pushed me first,
I lose my end: for here as well as I
A desperate may live, and a coward die.
Stag, dog, and all which from, or towards flies,
Is paid with life, or prey, or doing dies.
Fate grudges us all, and doth subtly lay
A scourge, 'gainst which we all forget to pray,
He that at sea prays for more wind, as well
Under the poles may beg cold, heat in hell.
What are we then? How little more alas
Is man now, than before he was! he was
Nothing; for us, we are for nothing fit;
Chance, or ourselves still disproportion it.
We have no power, no will, no sense; I lie,
I should not then thus feel this misery.

To Sir Henry Wotton

Sir, more than kisses, letters mingle souls;
For, thus friends absent speak. This ease controls
The tediousness of my life: but for these
I could ideate nothing, which could please,
But I should wither in one day, and pass
To a bottle of hay, that am a lock of grass.

Life is a voyage, and in our life's ways
Countries, courts, towns are rocks, or remoras;
They break or stop all ships, yet our state's such,
That though than pitch they stain worse, we must touch.
If in the furnace of the even line,
Or under th' adverse icy poles thou pine,
Thou know'st two temperate regions girded in,
Dwell there: But Oh, what refuge canst thou win
Parched in the Court, and in the country frozen?
Shall cities, built of both extremes, be chosen?
Can dung and garlic be a perfume? or can
A scorpion and torpedo cure a man?
Cities are worst of all three; of all three
(O knotty riddle) each is worst equally.
Cities are sepulchres; they who dwell there
Are carcases, as if no such there were.
And Courts are theatres, where some men play
Princes, some slaves, all to one end, and of one clay.
The country is a desert, where no good,
Gained (as habits, not born,) is understood.
There men become beasts, and prone to more evils;
In cities blocks, and in a lewd Court, devils.
As in the first Chaos confusedly
Each element's qualities were in the other three;
So pride, lust, covetize, being several
To these three places, yet all are in all,
And mingled thus, their issue incestuous.
Falsehood is denizened. Virtue is barbarous.
Let no man say there, 'Virtue's flinty wall
Shall lock vice in me, I'll do none, but know all.'
Men are sponges, which to pour out, receive,
Who know false play, rather than lose, deceive.
For in best understandings, sin began,
Angels sinned first, then devils, and then man.

Only perchance beasts sin not; wretched we
Are beasts in all, but white integrity.
I think if men, which in these places live
Durst look for themselves, and themselves retrieve,
They would like strangers greet themselves, seeing then
Utopian youth, grown old Italian.
  Be then thine own home, and in thyself dwell;
Inn anywhere, continuance maketh hell.
And seeing the snail, which everywhere doth roam,
Carrying his own house still, still is at home,
Follow (for he is easy paced) this snail,
Be thine own palace, or the world's thy gaol.
And in the world's sea, do not like cork sleep
Upon the water's face; nor in the deep
Sink like a lead without a line: but as
Fishes glide, leaving no print where they pass,
Nor making sound, so closely thy course go,
Let men dispute, whether thou breathe, or no.
Only in this one thing, be no Galenist: to make
Courts' hot ambitions wholesome, do not take
A dram of country's dullness; do not add
Correctives, but as chemics, purge the bad.
But, Sir, I advise not you, I rather do
Say o'er those lessons, which I learned of you:
Whom, free from German schisms, and lightness
Of France, and fair Italy's faithlessness,
Having from these sucked all they had of worth,
And brought home that faith, which you carried forth,
I throughly love. But if myself, I have won
To know my rules, I have, and you have

                              Donne.

His Picture (Elegy 5)

Here take my picture, though I bid farewell;
Thine, in my heart, where my soul dwells, shall dwell.
'Tis like me now, but I dead, 'twill be more
When we are shadows both, than 'twas before.
When weather-beaten I come back; my hand,
Perhaps with rude oars torn, or sun-beams tanned,
My face and breast of haircloth, and my head
With care's rash sudden hoariness o'erspread,
My body a sack of bones, broken within,
And powder's blue stains scattered on my skin;
If rival fools tax thee to have loved a man,
So foul, and coarse, as oh, I may seem then,
This shall say what I was: and thou shalt say,
Do his hurts reach me? doth my worth decay?
Or do they reach his judging mind, that he
Should now love less, what he did love to see?
That which in him was fair and delicate,
Was but the milk, which in love's childish state
Did nurse it: who now is grown strong enough
To feed on that, which to disused tastes seems tough.

On his Mistress (Elegy 16)

By our first strange and fatal interview,
By all desires which thereof did ensue,
By our long starving hopes, by that remorse
Which my words' masculine persuasive force
Begot in thee, and by the memory
Of hurts, which spies and rivals threatened me,
I calmly beg: but by thy father's wrath,
By all pains, which want and divorcement hath,

I conjure thee; and all the oaths which I
And thou have sworn to seal joint constancy,
Here I unswear, and overswear them thus,
Thou shalt not love by ways so dangerous.
Temper, O fair love, love's impetuous rage,
Be my true mistress still, not my feigned page;
I'll go, and, by thy kind leave, leave behind
Thee, only worthy to nurse in my mind
Thirst to come back; oh, if thou die before,
From other lands my soul towards thee shall soar,
Thy (else almighty) beauty cannot move
Rage from the seas, nor thy love teach them love,
Nor tame wild Boreas' harshness; thou hast read
How roughly he in pieces shivered
Fair Orithea, whom he swore he loved.
Fall ill or good, 'tis madness to have proved
Dangers unurged; feed on this flattery,
That absent lovers one in th' other be.
Dissemble nothing, not a boy, nor change
Thy body's habit, nor mind's; be not strange
To thy self only; all will spy in thy face
A blushing womanly discovering grace;
Richly clothed apes, are called apes, and as soon
Eclipsed as bright we call the moon the moon.
Men of France, changeable chameleons,
Spitals of diseases, shops of fashions,
Love's fuellers, and the rightest company
Of players, which upon the world's stage be,
Will quickly know thee, and know thee; and alas
Th' indifferent Italian, as we pass
His warm land, well content to think thee page,
Will hunt thee with such lust, and hideous rage,
As Lot's fair guests were vexed. But none of these
Nor spongy hydroptic Dutch shall thee displease,

If thou stay here. Oh stay here, for, for thee
England is only a worthy gallery,
To walk in expectation, till from thence
Our greatest King call thee to his presence.
When I am gone, dream me some happiness,
Nor let thy looks our long-hid love confess,
Nor praise, nor dispraise me, nor bless nor curse
Openly love's force, nor in bed fright thy nurse
With midnight's startings, crying out, 'Oh, oh
Nurse, O my love is slain, I saw him go
O'er the white Alps alone; I saw him, I,
Assailed, fight, taken, stabbed, bleed, fall, and die.'
Augur me better chance, except dread Jove
Think it enough for me to have had thy love.

The Dream

Dear love, for nothing less than thee
Would I have broke this happy dream,
        It was a theme
For reason, much too strong for phantasy,
Therefore thou waked'st me wisely; yet
My dream thou brok'st not, but continued'st it;
Thou art so true, that thoughts of thee suffice,
To make dreams truths, and fables histories;
Enter these arms, for since thou thought'st it best,
Not to dream all my dream, let's act the rest.

As lightning, or a taper's light,
Thine eyes, and not thy noise waked me;
        Yet I thought thee
(For thou lov'st truth) an angel, at first sight,
But when I saw thou saw'st my heart,

And knew'st my thoughts, beyond an angel's art,
When thou knew'st what I dreamed, when thou knew'st when
Excess of joy would wake me, and cam'st then,
I must confess, it could not choose but be
Profane, to think thee anything but thee.

Coming and staying showed thee, thee,
But rising makes me doubt, that now,
    Thou art not thou.
That love is weak, where fear's as strong as he;
'Tis not all spirit, pure, and brave,
If mixture it of fear, shame, honour, have.
Perchance as torches which must ready be,
Men light and put out, so thou deal'st with me,
Thou cam'st to kindle, goest to come; then I
Will dream that hope again, but else would die.

The Prohibition

Take heed of loving me,
At least remember, I forbade it thee;
  Not that I shall repair my unthrifty waste
Of breath and blood, upon thy sighs, and tears,
  By being to thee then what to me thou wast;
But, so great joy, our life at once outwears,
  Then, lest thy love, by my death, frustrate be,
  If thou love me, take heed of loving me.

Take heed of hating me,
Or too much triumph in the victory.
  Not that I shall be mine own officer,
And hate with hate again retaliate;
  But thou wilt lose the style of conqueror,

If I, thy conquest, perish by thy hate.
  Then, lest my being nothing lessen thee,
  If thou hate me, take heed of hating me.

    Yet, love and hate me too,
  So, these extremes shall neither's office do;
    Love me, that I may die the gentler way;
  Hate me, because thy love's too great for me;
    Or let these two, themselves, not me decay;
  So shall I live thy stage, not triumph be;
    Lest thou thy love and hate and me undo,
    To let me live, Oh love and hate me too.

The Canonization

For God's sake hold your tongue, and let me love,
  Or chide my palsy, or my gout,
My five grey hairs, or ruined fortune flout,
  With wealth your state, your mind with arts improve,
    Take you a course, get you a place,
    Observe his Honour, or his Grace,
Or the King's real, or his stamped face
  Contemplate; what you will, approve,
  So you will let me love.

Alas, alas, who's injured by my love?
  What merchant's ships have my sighs drowned?
Who says my tears have overflowed his ground?
  When did my colds a forward spring remove?
    When did the heats which my veins fill
    Add one more to the plaguy bill?
Soldiers find wars, and lawyers find out still

Litigious men, which quarrels move,
Though she and I do love.

Call us what you will, we are made such by love;
    Call her one, me another fly,
We are tapers too, and at our own cost die,
    And we in us find the eagle and the dove,
        The phoenix riddle hath more wit
        By us; we two being one, are it.
So to one neutral thing both sexes fit
    We die and rise the same, and prove
    Mysterious by this love.

We can die by it, if not live by love,
    And if unfit for tombs and hearse
Our legend be, it will be fit for verse;
    And if no piece of chronicle we prove,
        We'll build in sonnets pretty rooms;
        As well a well wrought urn becomes
The greatest ashes, as half-acre tombs,
    And by these hymns, all shall approve
    Us canonized for love:

And thus invoke us; 'You whom reverend love
    Made one another's hermitage;
You, to whom love was peace, that now is rage;
    Who did the whole world's soul contract, and drove
        Into the glasses of your eyes
        (So made such mirrors, and such spies,
That they did all to you epitomize,)
    Countries, towns, courts: beg from above
    A pattern of your love!'

Air and Angels

Twice or thrice had I loved thee,
Before I knew thy face or name;
So in a voice, so in a shapeless flame,
Angels affect us oft, and worshipped be;
    Still when, to where thou wert, I came,
Some lovely glorious nothing I did see,
    But since my soul, whose child love is,
Takes limbs of flesh, and else could nothing do,
    More subtle than the parent is
Love must not be, but take a body too,
    And therefore what thou wert, and who
        I bid love ask, and now
That it assume thy body, I allow,
And fix itself in thy lip, eye, and brow.

Whilst thus to ballast love, I thought,
And so more steadily to have gone,
With wares which would sink admiration,
I saw, I had love's pinnace overfraught,
    Every thy hair for love to work upon
Is much too much, some fitter must be sought;
    For, nor in nothing, nor in things
Extreme, and scatt'ring bright, can love inhere;
    Then as an angel, face and wings
Of air, not pure as it, yet pure doth wear,
    So thy love may be my love's sphere;
        Just such disparity
As is 'twixt air and angels' purity,
'Twixt women's love, and men's will ever be.

The Ecstasy

Where, like a pillow on a bed,
    A pregnant bank swelled up, to rest
The violet's reclining head,
    Sat we two, one another's best;

Our hands were firmly cemented
    With a fast balm, which thence did spring,
Our eye-beams twisted, and did thread
    Our eyes, upon one double string;

So to'intergraft our hands, as yet
    Was all our means to make us one,
And pictures in our eyes to get
    Was all our propagation.

As 'twixt two equal armies, Fate
    Suspends uncertain victory,
Our souls, (which to advance their state,
    Were gone out), hung 'twixt her, and me.

And whilst our souls negotiate there,
    We like sepulchral statues lay;
All day, the same our postures were,
    And we said nothing, all the day.

If any, so by love refined,
    That he soul's language understood,
And by good love were grown all mind,
    Within convenient distance stood,

He (though he knew not which soul spake
    Because both meant, both spake the same)

Might thence a new concoction take,
  And part far purer than he came.

This ecstasy doth unperplex
  (We said) and tell us what we love,
We see by this, it was not sex,
  We see, we saw not what did move:

But as all several souls contain
  Mixture of things, they know not what,
Love, these mixed souls doth mix again,
  And makes both one, each this and that.

A single violet transplant,
  The strength, the colour, and the size,
(All which before was poor, and scant,)
  Redoubles still, and multiplies.

When love, with one another so
  Interinanimates two souls,
That abler soul, which thence doth flow,
  Defects of loneliness controls.

We then, who are this new soul, know,
  Of what we are composed, and made,
For, th' atomies of which we grow,
  Are souls, whom no change can invade.

But O alas, so long, so far
  Our bodies why do we forbear?
They are ours, though they are not we, we are
  The intelligences, they the sphere.

We owe them thanks, because they thus,
    Did us, to us, at first convey,
Yielded their forces, sense, to us,
    Nor are dross to us, but allay.

On man heaven's influence works not so,
    But that it first imprints the air,
So soul into the soul may flow,
    Though it to body first repair.

As our blood labours to beget
    Spirits, as like souls as it can,
Because such fingers need to knit
    That subtle knot, which makes us man:

So must pure lovers' souls descend
    T' affections, and to faculties,
Which sense may reach and apprehend,
    Else a great prince in prison lies.

To our bodies turn we then, that so
    Weak men on love revealed may look;
Love's mysteries in souls do grow,
    But yet the body is his book.

And if some lover, such as we,
    Have heard this dialogue of one,
Let him still mark us, he shall see
    Small change, when we'are to bodies gone.

A Fever

Oh do not die, for I shall hate
   All women so, when thou art gone,
That thee I shall not celebrate,
   When I remember, thou wast one.

But yet thou canst not die, I know,
   To leave this world behind, is death,
But when thou from this world wilt go,
   The whole world vapours with thy breath.

Or if, when thou, the world's soul, go'st,
   It stay, 'tis but thy carcase then,
The fairest woman, but thy ghost,
   But corrupt worms, the worthiest men.

Oh wrangling schools, that search what fire
   Shall burn this world, had none the wit
Unto this knowledge to aspire,
   That this her fever might be it?

And yet she cannot waste by this,
   Nor long bear this torturing wrong,
For much corruption needful is
   To fuel such a fever long.

These burning fits but meteors be,
   Whose matter in thee is soon spent.
Thy beauty, and all parts, which are thee,
   Are unchangeable firmament.

Yet 'twas of my mind, seizing thee,
   Though it in thee cannot perséver.

For I had rather owner be
　　Of thee one hour, than all else ever.

Lovers' Infiniteness

If yet I have not all thy love,
Dear, I shall never have it all,
I cannot breathe one other sigh, to move,
Nor can entreat one other tear to fall.
All my treasure, which should purchase thee,
Sighs, tears, and oaths, and letters I have spent,
Yet no more can be due to me,
Than at the bargain made was meant.
If then thy gift of love were partial,
That some to me, some should to others fall,
　　Dear, I shall never have thee all.

Or if then thou gavest me all,
All was but all, which thou hadst then;
But if in thy heart, since, there be or shall
New love created be, by other men,
Which have their stocks entire, and can in tears,
In sighs, in oaths, and letters outbid me,
This new love may beget new fears,
For, this love was not vowed by thee.
And yet it was, thy gift being general,
The ground, thy heart is mine; whatever shall
　　Grow there, dear, I should have it all.

Yet I would not have all yet,
He that hath all can have no more,
And since my love doth every day admit
New growth, thou shouldst have new rewards in store;

Thou canst not every day give me thy heart,
If thou canst give it, then thou never gav'st it:
Love's riddles are, that though thy heart depart,
It stays at home, and thou with losing sav'st it:
But we will have a way more liberal,
Than changing hearts, to join them, so we shall
    Be one, and one another's all.

The Anniversary

All kings, and all their favourites,
  All glory of honours, beauties, wits,
The sun itself, which makes times, as they pass,
Is elder by a year, now, than it was
When thou and I first one another saw:
All other things, to their destruction draw,
    Only our love hath no decay;
This, no tomorrow hath, nor yesterday,
Running it never runs from us away,
But truly keeps his first, last, everlasting day.

Two graves must hide thine and my corse,
  If one might, death were no divorce,
Alas, as well as other princes, we,
(Who prince enough in one another be,)
Must leave at last in death, these eyes, and ears,
Oft fed with true oaths, and with sweet salt tears;
    But souls where nothing dwells but love
(All other thoughts being inmates) then shall prove
This, or a love increased there above,
When bodies to their graves, souls from their graves remove.

And then we shall be throughly blessed,
    But we no more, than all the rest.
Here upon earth, we are kings, and none but we
Can be such kings, nor of such subjects be;
Who is so safe as we? where none can do
Treason to us, except one of us two.
    True and false fears let us refrain,
Let us love nobly, and live, and add again
Years and years unto years, till we attain
To write threescore, this is the second of our reign.

A Valediction: of Weeping

    Let me pour forth
My tears before thy face, whilst I stay here,
For thy face coins them, and thy stamp they bear,
And by this mintage they are something worth,
    For thus they be
    Pregnant of thee;
Fruits of much grief they are, emblems of more,
When a tear falls, that thou falls which it bore,
So thou and I are nothing then, when on a divers shore.

    On a round ball
A workman that hath copies by, can lay
An Europe, Afric, and an Asia,
And quickly make that, which was nothing, all,
    So doth each tear,
    Which thee doth wear,
A globe, yea world by that impression grow,
Till thy tears mixed with mine do overflow
This world, by waters sent from thee, my heaven dissolved so.

O more than moon,
Draw not up seas to drown me in thy sphere,
Weep me not dead, in thine arms, but forbear
To teach the sea, what it may do too soon;
    Let not the wind
    Example find,
To do me more harm, than it purposeth;
Since thou and I sigh one another's breath,
Whoe'er sighs most, is cruellest, and hastes the other's death.

Song

Sweetest love, I do not go,
    For weariness of thee,
Nor in hope the world can show
    A fitter love for me;
      But since that I
Must die at last, 'tis best,
To use my self in jest
    Thus by feigned deaths to die.

Yesternight the sun went hence,
    And yet is here today,
He hath no desire nor sense,
    Nor half so short a way:
      Then fear not me,
But believe that I shall make
Speedier journeys, since I take
    More wings and spurs than he.

O how feeble is man's power,
    That if good fortune fall,
Cannot add another hour,

Nor a lost hour recall!
    But come bad chance,
And we join to it our strength,
And we teach it art and length,
    Itself o'er us to advance.

When thou sigh'st, thou sigh'st not wind,
    But sigh'st my soul away,
When thou weep'st, unkindly kind,
    My life's blood doth decay.
      It cannot be
That thou lov'st me, as thou say'st,
If in thine my life thou waste,
    Thou art the best of me.

Let not thy divining heart
    Forethink me any ill,
Destiny may take thy part,
    And may thy fears fulfil;
      But think that we
Are but turned aside to sleep;
They who one another keep
    Alive, ne'er parted be.

A Valediction: forbidding Mourning

As virtuous men pass mildly away,
    And whisper to their souls, to go,
Whilst some of their sad friends do say,
    The breath goes now, and some say, no:

So let us melt, and make no noise,
    No tear-floods, nor sigh-tempests move,

'Twere profanation of our joys
   To tell the laity our love.

Moving of th' earth brings harms and fears,
   Men reckon what it did and meant,
But trepidation of the spheres,
   Though greater far, is innocent.

Dull sublunary lovers' love
   (Whose soul is sense) cannot admit
Absence, because it doth remove
   Those things which elemented it.

But we by a love, so much refined,
   That our selves know not what it is,
Inter-assured of the mind,
   Care less, eyes, lips, and hands to miss.

Our two souls therefore, which are one,
   Though I must go, endure not yet
A breach, but an expansion,
   Like gold to aery thinness beat.

If they be two, they are two so
   As stiff twin compasses are two,
Thy soul the fixed foot, makes no show
   To move, but doth, if th'other do.

And though it in the centre sit,
   Yet when the other far doth roam,
It leans, and hearkens after it,
   And grows erect, as that comes home.

Such wilt thou be to me, who must
    Like th' other foot, obliquely run;
Thy firmness makes my circle just,
    And makes me end, where I begun.

The Undertaking

I have done one braver thing
    Than all the Worthies did,
And yet a braver thence doth spring,
    Which is, to keep that hid.

It were but madness now t'impart
    The skill of specular stone,
When he which can have learned the art
    To cut it, can find none.

So, if I now should utter this,
    Others (because no more
Such stuff to work upon, there is,)
    Would love but as before.

But he who loveliness within
    Hath found, all outward loathes,
For he who colour loves, and skin,
    Loves but their oldest clothes.

If, as I have, you also do
    Virtue attired in woman see,
And dare love that, and say so too,
    And forget the He and She;

And if this love, though placed so,
    From profane men you hide,
Which will no faith on this bestow,
    Or, if they do, deride:

Then you have done a braver thing
    Than all the Worthies did,
And a braver thence will spring,
    Which is, to keep that hid.

The Funeral

Whoever comes to shroud me, do not harm
        Nor question much
That subtle wreath of hair, which crowns my arm;
The mystery, the sign you must not touch,
        For 'tis my outward soul,
Viceroy to that, which then to heaven being gone,
        Will leave this to control,
And keep these limbs, her provinces, from dissolution.

For if the sinewy thread my brain lets fall
        Through every part,
Can tie those parts, and make me one of all;
These hairs which upward grew, and strength and art
        Have from a better brain,
Can better do it; except she meant that I
        By this should know my pain,
As prisoners then are manacled, when they are condemned to
    die.

Whate'er she meant by it, bury it with me,
        For since I am

Love's martyr, it might breed idolatry,
If into others' hands these relics came;
　　　As 'twas humility
To afford to it all that a soul can do,
　　　So, 'tis some bravery,
That since you would save none of me, I bury some of you.

The Relic

　　　When my grave is broke up again
　　　Some second guest to entertain,
　　　(For graves have learned that woman-head
　　　To be to more than one a bed)
　　　　　And he that digs it, spies
A bracelet of bright hair about the bone,
　　　　　Will he not let us alone,
And think that there a loving couple lies,
Who thought that this device might be some way
To make their souls, at the last busy day,
Meet at this grave, and make a little stay?

　　　If this fall in a time, or land,
　　　Where mis-devotion doth command,
　　　Then, he that digs us up, will bring
　　　Us, to the Bishop, and the King,
　　　　　To make us relics; then
Thou shalt be a Mary Magdalen, and I
　　　　　A something else thereby;
All women shall adore us, and some men;
And since at such time, miracles are sought,
I would have that age by this paper taught
What miracles we harmless lovers wrought.

First, we loved well and faithfully,
Yet knew not what we loved, nor why,
Difference of sex no more we knew,
Than our guardian angels do;
        Coming and going, we
Perchance might kiss, but not between those meals;
        Our hands ne'er touched the seals,
Which nature, injured by late law, sets free:
These miracles we did; but now alas,
All measure, and all language, I should pass,
Should I tell what a miracle she was.

Twicknam Garden

Blasted with sighs, and surrounded with tears,
    Hither I come to seek the spring,
    And at mine eyes, and at mine ears,
Receive such balms, as else cure everything;
    But O, self traitor, I do bring
The spider love, which transubstantiates all,
    And can convert manna to gall,
And that this place may thoroughly be thought
    True paradise, I have the serpent brought.

'Twere wholesomer for me, that winter did
    Benight the glory of this place,
    And that a grave frost did forbid
These trees to laugh, and mock me to my face;
    But that I may not this disgrace
Endure, nor yet leave loving, Love, let me
    Some senseless piece of this place be;
Make me a mandrake, so I may groan here,
    Or a stone fountain weeping out my year.

Hither with crystal vials, lovers come,
    And take my tears, which are love's wine,
And try your mistress' tears at home,
For all are false, that taste not just like mine;
    Alas, hearts do not in eyes shine,
Nor can you more judge woman's thoughts by tears,
    Than by her shadow, what she wears.
O perverse sex, where none is true but she,
    Who's therefore true, because her truth kills me.

A Lecture upon the Shadow

Stand still, and I will read to thee
A lecture, love, in love's philosophy.
        These three hours that we have spent,
        Walking here, two shadows went
Along with us, which we ourselves produced;
But, now the sun is just above our head,
        We do those shadows tread;
        And to brave clearness all things are reduced.
    So whilst our infant loves did grow,
    Disguises did, and shadows, flow,
    From us, and our care; but, now 'tis not so.

That love hath not attained the high'st degree,
Which is still diligent lest others see.

Except our loves at this noon stay,
We shall new shadows make the other way.
        As the first were made to blind
        Others; these which come behind
Will work upon ourselves, and blind our eyes.
If our loves faint, and westwardly decline;

To me thou, falsely, thine,
    And I to thee mine actions shall disguise.
The morning shadows wear away,
But these grow longer all the day,
    But oh, love's day is short, if love decay.

Love is a growing, or full constant light;
And his first minute, after noon, is night.

A Nocturnal upon S. Lucy's Day, being the shortest day

'Tis the year's midnight, and it is the day's,
Lucy's, who scarce seven hours herself unmasks,
    The sun is spent, and now his flasks
    Send forth light squibs, no constant rays;
        The world's whole sap is sunk:
The general balm th' hydroptic earth hath drunk,
Whither, as to the bed's-feet, life is shrunk,
Dead and interred; yet all these seem to laugh,
Compared with me, who am their epitaph.

Study me then, you who shall lovers be
At the next world, that is, at the next spring:
    For I am every dead thing,
    In whom love wrought new alchemy.
        For his art did express
A quintessence even from nothingness,
From dull privations, and lean emptiness
He ruined me, and I am re-begot
Of absence, darkness, death; things which are not.

All others, from all things, draw all that's good,
Life, soul, form, spirit, whence they being have;

I, by love's limbeck, am the grave
Of all, that's nothing. Oft a flood
Have we two wept, and so
Drowned the whole world, us two; oft did we grow
To be two chaoses, when we did show
Care to aught else; and often absences
Withdrew our souls, and made us carcases.

But I am by her death (which word wrongs her)
Of the first nothing, the elixir grown;
Were I a man, that I were one,
I needs must know; I should prefer,
If I were any beast,
Some ends, some means; yea plants, yea stones detest,
And love; all, all some properties invest;
If I an ordinary nothing were,
As shadow, a light, and body must be here.

But I am none; nor will my sun renew.
You lovers, for whose sake, the lesser sun
At this time to the Goat is run
To fetch new lust, and give it you,
Enjoy your summer all;
Since she enjoys her long night's festival,
Let me prepare towards her, and let me call
This hour her vigil, and her eve, since this
Both the year's, and the day's deep midnight is.

The Autumnal (Elegy 9)

No spring, nor summer beauty hath such grace,
As I have seen in one autumnal face.
Young beauties force your love, and that's a rape,

This doth but counsel, yet you cannot scape.
If 'twere a shame to love, here 'twere no shame,
    Affection here takes reverence's name.
Were her first years the Golden Age; that's true,
    But now she's gold oft tried, and ever new.
That was her torrid and inflaming time,
    This is her tolerable tropic clime.
Fair eyes, who asks more heat than comes from hence,
    He in a fever wishes pestilence.
Call not these wrinkles, graves; if graves they were,
    They were Love's graves; for else he is no where.
Yet lies not Love dead here, but here doth sit
    Vowed to this trench, like an anachorit.
And here, till hers, which must be his death, come,
    He doth not dig a grave, but build a tomb.
Here dwells he, though he sojourn everywhere,
    In Progress, yet his standing house is here.
Here, where still evening is; not noon, nor night;
    Where no voluptuousness, yet all delight.
In all her words, unto all hearers fit,
    You may at revels, you at council, sit.
This is Love's timber, youth his underwood;
    There he, as wine in June, enrages blood,
Which then comes seasonabliest, when our taste
    And appetite to other things is past.
Xerxes' strange Lydian love, the platan tree,
    Was loved for age, none being so large as she,
Or else because, being young, nature did bless
    Her youth with age's glory, barrenness.
If we love things long sought, age is a thing
    Which we are fifty years in compassing.
If transitory things, which soon decay,
    Age must be loveliest at the latest day.
But name not winter-faces, whose skin's slack;

Lank, as an unthrift's purse; but a soul's sack;
Whose eyes seek light within, for all here's shade;
    Whose mouths are holes, rather worn out, than made;
Whose every tooth to a several place is gone,
    To vex their souls at Resurrection;
Name not these living death's-heads unto me,
    For these, not ancient, but antiques be.
I hate extremes; yet I had rather stay
    With tombs, than cradles, to wear out a day.
Since such love's natural lation is, may still
    My love descend, and journey down the hill,
Not panting after growing beauties, so,
    I shall ebb out with them, who homeward go.

II. FROM *THE ANNIVERSARIES*

An Anatomy of the World

THE FIRST ANNIVERSARY

. . . .
There is no health; physicians say that we   *Impossibility of health.*
At best, enjoy but a neutrality.
And can there be worse sickness, than to know
That we are never well, nor can be so?
We are born ruinous: poor mothers cry,
That children come not right, nor orderly,
Except they headlong come, and fall upon
An ominous precipitation.
How witty's ruin! how importunate
Upon mankind! it laboured to frustrate
Even God's purpose; and made woman, sent
For man's relief, cause of his languishment.
They were to good ends, and they are so still,
But accessory, and principal in ill.
For that first marriage was our funeral:
One woman at one blow, then killed us all,
And singly, one by one, they kill us now.
We do delightfully ourselves allow
To that consumption; and profusely blind,
We kill ourselves, to propagate our kind.
. . . .
With new diseases on ourselves we war,

And with new physic, a worse engine far.
Thus man, this world's vice-emperor, in whom
All faculties, all graces are at home;
And if in other creatures they appear,
They're but man's ministers, and legates there,
To work on their rebellions, and reduce
Them to civility, and to man's use.
This man, whom God did woo, and loth t' attend
Till man came up, did down to man descend,
This man, so great, that all that is, is his,
Oh what a trifle, and poor thing he is!
If man were anything, he's nothing now:
Help, or at least some time to waste, allow
T' his other wants, yet when he did depart
With her whom we lament, he lost his heart.
She, of whom th' ancients seemed to prophesy,
When they called virtues by the name of *she;*
She in whom virtue was so much refined,
That for allay unto so pure a mind
She took the weaker sex, she that could drive
The poisonous tincture, and the stain of Eve,
Out of her thoughts, and deeds; and purify
All, by a true religious alchemy;
She, she is dead; she's dead: when thou know'st this,
Thou know'st how poor a trifling thing man is.
And learn'st thus much by our anatomy,
The heart being perished, no part can be free.
And that except thou feed (not banquet) on
The supernatural food, religion,
Thy better growth grows withered, and scant;
Be more than man, or thou'art less than an ant.
Then, as mankind, so is the world's whole frame
Quite out of joint, almost created lame:
For, before God had made up all the rest,

Corruption entered, and depraved the best:
It seized the angels, and then first of all
The world did in her cradle take a fall,
And turned her brains, and took a general maim
Wronging each joint of th' universal frame.
The noblest part, man, felt it first; and then
Both beasts and plants, cursed in the curse of man.
So did the world from the first hour decay,
That evening was beginning of the day,
And now the springs and summers which we see,
Like sons of women after fifty be.
And new philosophy calls all in doubt,
The element of fire is quite put out;
The sun is lost, and th' earth, and no man's wit
Can well direct him where to look for it.
And freely men confess that this world's spent,
When in the planets, and the firmament
They seek so many new; they see that this
Is crumbled out again to his atomies.
'Tis all in pieces, all coherence gone;
All just supply, and all relation:
Prince, subject, father, son, are things forgot,
For every man alone thinks he hath got
To be a phoenix, and that then can be
None of that kind, of which he is, but he.
This is the world's condition now, and now
She that should all parts to reunion bow,
She that had all magnetic force alone,
To draw, and fasten sundered parts in one;
She whom wise nature had invented then
When she observed that every sort of men
Did in their voyage in this world's sea stray,
And needed a new compass for their way;
She that was best, and first original

*Decay of
nature in
other
parts.*

Of all fair copies; and the general
Steward to Fate; she whose rich eyes, and breast,
Gilt the West Indies, and perfumed the East;
Whose having breathed in this world, did bestow
Spice on those isles, and bade them still smell so,
And that rich Indy which doth gold inter,
Is but as single money, coined from her:
She to whom this world must itself refer,
As suburbs, or the microcosm of her,
She, she is dead; she's dead: when thou know'st this,
Thou know'st how lame a cripple this world is.
And learn'st thus much by our anatomy,
That this world's general sickness doth not lie
In any humour, or one certain part;
But as thou sawest it rotten at the heart,
Thou seest a hectic fever hath got hold
Of the whole substance, not to be controlled,
And that thou hast but one way, not to admit
The world's infection, to be none of it.
For the world's subtlest immaterial parts
Feel this consuming wound, and age's darts.
For the world's beauty is decayed, or gone,   *Disformity of parts.*
Beauty, that's colour, and proportion.
We think the heavens enjoy their spherical,
Their round proportion embracing all.
But yet their various and perplexed course,
Observed in divers ages, doth enforce
Men to find out so many eccentric parts,
Such divers down-right lines, such overthwarts,
As disproportion that pure form. It tears
The firmament in eight and forty shares,
And in these constellations then arise
New stars, and old do vanish from our eyes:
As though heaven suffered earthquakes, peace or war,

When new towers rise, and old demolished are.
They have impaled within a zodiac
The free-born sun, and keep twelve signs awake
To watch his steps; the goat and crab control,
And fright him back, who else to either pole
(Did not these tropics fetter him) might run:
For his course is not round; nor can the sun
Perfect a circle, or maintain his way
One inch direct; but where he rose today
He comes no more, but with a cozening line,
Steals by that point, and so is serpentine:
And seeming weary with his reeling thus,
He means to sleep, being now fall'n nearer us.
So, of the stars which boast that they do run
In circle still, none ends where he begun.
All their proportion's lame, it sinks, it swells.
For of meridians, and parallels,
Man hath weaved out a net, and this net thrown
Upon the heavens, and now they are his own.
Loth to go up the hill, or labour thus
To go to heaven, we make heaven come to us.
We spur, we rein the stars, and in their race
They're diversely content t' obey our pace.
But keeps the earth her round proportion still?
Doth not a Tenerife, or higher hill
Rise so high like a rock, that one might think
The floating moon would shipwreck there, and sink?
Seas are so deep, that whales being struck today,
Perchance tomorrow, scarce at middle way
Of their wished journey's end, the bottom, die.
And men, to sound depths, so much line untie,
As one might justly think that there would rise
At end thereof, one of th' Antipodes:
If under all, a vault infernal be,

(Which sure is spacious, except that we
Invent another torment, that there must
Millions into a strait hot room be thrust)
Then solidness, and roundness have no place.
Are these but warts, and pock-holes in the face
Of th' earth? Think so: but yet confess, in this
The world's proportion disfigured is,
That those two legs whereon it doth rely,   *Disorder in the world.*
Reward and punishment are bent awry.
And, oh, it can no more be questioned,
That beauty's best, proportion, is dead,
Since even grief itself, which now alone
Is left us, is without proportion.
She by whose lines proportion should be
Examined, measure of all symmetry,
Whom had that ancient seen, who thought souls made
Of harmony, he would at next have said
That harmony was she, and thence infer,
That souls were but resultances from her,
And did from her into our bodies go,
As to our eyes, the forms from objects flow:
She, who if those great Doctors truly said
That the Ark to man's proportions was made,
Had been a type for that, as that might be
A type of her in this, that contrary
Both elements, and passions lived at peace
In her, who caused all civil war to cease.
She, after whom, what form soe'er we see,
Is discord, and rude incongruity;
She, she is dead, she's dead; when thou know'st this
Thou know'st how ugly a monster this world is:
And learn'st thus much by our anatomy,
That here is nothing to enamour thee:
And that, not only faults in inward parts,

Corruptions in our brains, or in our hearts,
Poisoning the fountains, whence our actions spring,
Endanger us: but that if everything
Be not done fitly'and in proportion,
To satisfy wise, and good lookers on,
(Since most men be such as most think they be)
They're loathsome too, by this deformity.
For good, and well, must in our actions meet;
Wicked is not much worse than indiscreet.
But beauty's other second element,
Colour, and lustre now, is as near spent.
And had the world his just proportion,
Were it a ring still, yet the stone is gone.
As a compassionate turquoise which doth tell
By looking pale, the wearer is not well,
As gold falls sick being stung with mercury,
All the world's parts of such complexion be.
When nature was most busy, the first week,
Swaddling the new born earth, God seemed to like
That she should sport herself sometimes, and play,
To mingle, and vary colours every day:
And then, as though she could not make enow,
Himself his various rainbow did allow.
Sight is the noblest sense of any one,
Yet sight hath only colour to feed on,
And colour is decayed: summer's robe grows
Dusky, and like an oft dyed garment shows.
Our blushing red, which used in cheeks to spread,
Is inward sunk, and only our souls are red.
Perchance the world might have recovered,
If she whom we lament had not been dead:
But she, in whom all white, and red, and blue
(Beauty's ingredients) voluntary grew,
As in an unvexed paradise; from whom

Did all things verdure, and their lustre come,
Whose composition was miraculous,
Being all colour, all diaphanous,
(For air, and fire but thick gross bodies were,
And liveliest stones but drowsy, and pale to her,)
She, she is dead; she's dead: when thou know'st this,
Thou know'st how wan a ghost this our world is:
And learn'st thus much by our anatomy,
That it should more affright, than pleasure thee.
. . . .
Since herbs, and roots by dying, lose not all,
But they, yea ashes too, are medicinal,
Death could not quench her virtue so, but that
It would be (if not followed) wondered at:
And all the world would be one dying swan,
To sing her funeral praise, and vanish then.
But as some serpents' poison hurteth not,
Except it be from the live serpent shot,
So doth her virtue need her here, to fit
That unto us; she working more than it.
But she, in whom to such maturity
Virtue was grown, past growth, that it must die,
She, from whose influence all impressions came,
But, by receivers' impotencies, lame,
Who, though she could not transubstantiate
All states to gold, yet gilded every state,
So that some princes have some temperance;
Some counsellors some purpose to advance
The common profit; and some people have
Some stay, no more than kings should give, to crave;
Some women have some taciturnity,
Some nunneries, some grains of chastity.
She that did thus much, and much more could do,
But that our age was iron, and rusty too,

She, she is dead; she's dead; when thou know'st this,
Thou know'st how dry a cinder this world is.
And learn'st thus much by our anatomy,
That 'tis in vain to dew, or mollify
It with thy tears, or sweat, or blood: nothing
Is worth our travail, grief, or perishing,
But those rich joys, which did possess her heart,
Of which she's now partaker, and a part.
But as in cutting up a man that's dead,   *Conclusion.*
The body will not last out to have read
On every part, and therefore men direct
Their speech to parts, that are of most effect;
So the world's carcase would not last, if I
Were punctual in this anatomy.
Nor smells it well to hearers, if one tell
Them their disease, who fain would think they're well.
Here therefore be the end: and, blessed maid,
Of whom is meant whatever hath been said,
Or shall be spoken well by any tongue,
Whose name refines coarse lines, and makes prose song,
Accept this tribute, and his first year's rent,
Who till his dark short taper's end be spent,
As oft as thy feast sees this widowed earth,
Will yearly celebrate thy second birth,
That is, thy death. For though the soul of man
Be got when man is made, 'tis born but then
When man doth die. Our body's as the womb,
And as a midwife death directs it home.
And you her creatures, whom she works upon
And have your last, and best concoction
From her example, and her virtue, if you
In reverence to her, do think it due,
That no one should her praises thus rehearse,
As matter fit for chronicle, not verse,

Vouchsafe to call to mind, that God did make
A last, and lasting'st piece, a song. He spake
To Moses, to deliver unto all,
That song: because he knew they would let fall
The Law, the prophets, and the history,
But keep the song still in their memory.
Such an opinion (in due measure) made
Me this great office boldly to invade.
Nor could incomprehensibleness deter
Me, from thus trying to emprison her.
Which when I saw that a strict grave could do,
I saw not why verse might not do so too.
Verse hath a middle nature: heaven keeps souls,
The grave keeps bodies, verse the fame enrols.

Of the Progress of the Soul

THE SECOND ANNIVERSARY

Nothing could make me sooner to confess   *The entrance.*
That this world had an everlastingness,
Than to consider, that a year is run,
Since both this lower world's and the sun's sun,
The lustre, and the vigour of this all,
Did set; 'twere blasphemy to say, did fall.
But as a ship which hath struck sail, doth run
By force of that force which before, it won:
Or as sometimes in a beheaded man,
Though at those two red seas, which freely ran,
One from the trunk, another from the head,
His soul be sailed, to her eternal bed,
His eyes will twinkle, and his tongue will roll,
As though he beckoned, and called back his soul,

He grasps his hands, and he pulls up his feet,
And seems to reach, and to step forth to meet
His soul; when all these motions which we saw,
Are but as ice, which crackles at a thaw:
Or as a lute, which in moist weather, rings
Her knell alone, by cracking of her strings:
So struggles this dead world, now she is gone;
For there is motion in corruption.
As some days are, at the Creation named,
Before the sun, the which framed days, was framed,
So after this sun's set, some show appears,
And orderly vicissitude of years.
Yet a new Deluge, and of Lethe flood,
Hath drowned us all, all have forgot all good,
Forgetting her, the main reserve of all,
Yet in this deluge, gross and general,
Thou seest me strive for life; my life shall be,
To be hereafter praised, for praising thee,
Immortal Maid, who though thou would'st refuse
The name of mother, be unto my Muse
A father, since her chaste ambition is,
Yearly to bring forth such a child as this.
These hymns may work on future wits, and so
May great grandchildren of thy praises grow.
And so, though not revive, embalm and spice
The world, which else would putrefy with vice.
For thus, man may extend thy progeny,
Until man do but vanish, and not die.
These hymns thy issue, may increase so long,
As till God's great *Venite* change the song.
Thirst for that time, O my insatiate soul,
And serve thy thirst, with God's safe-sealing bowl.
Be thirsty still, and drink still till thou go;
'Tis th' only health, to be hydroptic so.

*A just
disestimation
of the world.*

Forget this rotten world; and unto thee
Let thine own times as an old story be.
Be not concerned: study not why, nor when;
Do not so much, as not believe a man.
For though to err, be worst, to try truths forth,
Is far more business than this world is worth.
The world is but a carcase; thou art fed
By it, but as a worm, that carcase bred;
And why shouldst thou, poor worm, consider more,
When this world will grow better than before,
Than those thy fellow worms do think upon
That carcase's last resurrection.
Forget this world, and scarce think of it so,
As of old clothes, cast off a year ago.
To be thus stupid is alacrity;
Men thus lethargic have best memory.
Look upward; that's towards her, whose happy state
We now lament not, but congratulate.
She, to whom all this world was but a stage,
Where all sat hearkening how her youthful age
Should be employed, because in all she did,
Some figure of the Golden Times was hid;
Who could not lack, whate'er this world could give,
Because she was the form, that made it live;
Nor could complain, that this world was unfit
To be stayed in, then when she was in it;
She that first tried indifferent desires
By virtue, and virtue by religious fires,
She to whose person Paradise adhered,
As Courts to princes, she whose eyes ensphered
Star-light enough, to' have made the south control,
(Had she been there) the star-full northern pole,
She, she is gone; she is gone; when thou know'st this,
What fragmentary rubbish this world is

Thou know'st, and that it is not worth a thought; *Contemplation*
He honours it too much that thinks it naught. *of our state in*
Think then, my soul, that death is but a groom, *our deathbed.*
Which brings a taper to the outward room,
Whence thou spiest first a little glimmering light,
And after brings it nearer to thy sight:
For such approaches doth heaven make in death.
Think thyself labouring now with broken breath,
And think those broken and soft notes to be
Division, and thy happiest harmony.
Think thee laid on thy death-bed, loose and slack;
And think that, but unbinding of a pack,
To take one precious thing, thy soul, from thence.
Think thyself parched with fever's violence,
Anger thine ague more, by calling it
Thy physic; chide the slackness of the fit.
Think that thou hear'st thy knell, and think no more,
But that, as bells called thee to church before,
So this, to the Triumphant Church, calls thee.
Think Satan's sergeants round about thee be,
And think that but for legacies they thrust;
Give one thy pride, to another give thy lust:
Give them those sins which they gave thee before,
And trust th' immaculate blood to wash thy score.
Think thy friends weeping round, and think that they
Weep but because they go not yet thy way.
Think that they close thine eyes, and think in this,
That they confess much in the world, amiss,
Who dare not trust a dead man's eye with that,
Which they from God, and angels cover not.
Think that they shroud thee up, and think from thence
They reinvest thee in white innocence.
Think that thy body rots, and (if so low,
Thy soul exalted so, thy thoughts can go),

Think thee a prince, who of themselves create
Worms which insensibly devour their state.
Think that they bury thee, and think that rite
Lays thee to sleep but a Saint Lucy's night.
Think these things cheerfully: and if thou be
Drowsy or slack, remember then that she,
She whose complexion was so even made,
That which of her ingredients should invade
The other three, no fear, no art could guess:
So far were all removed from more or less.
But as in mithridate, or just perfumes,
Where all good things being met, no one presumes
To govern, or to triumph on the rest,
Only because all were, no part was best.
. . . .
She, she embraced a sickness, gave it meat,
The purest blood, and breath, that e'er it eat;
And hath taught us, that though a good man hath
Title to heaven, and plead it by his faith,
And though he may pretend a conquest, since
Heaven was content to suffer violence,
Yea though he plead a long possession too,
(For they're in heaven on earth who heaven's works do)
Though he had right, and power, and place before,
Yet death must usher, and unlock the door.
Think further on thy self, my soul, and think
How thou at first was made but in a sink;
Think that it argued some infirmity,   *Incom-*
That those two souls, which then thou found'st in me,   *modities*
Thou fed'st upon, and drew'st into thee, both   *of the*
My second soul of sense, and first of growth.   *soul in*
Think but how poor thou wast, how obnoxious;   *the body.*
Whom a small lump of flesh could poison thus.
This curded milk, this poor unlittered whelp

My body, could, beyond escape or help,
Infect thee with original sin, and thou
Couldst neither then refuse, nor leave it now.
Think that no stubborn sullen anchorite,
Which fixed to a pillar, or a grave doth sit
Bedded, and bathed in all his ordures, dwells
So foully as our souls in their first-built cells.
Think in how poor a prison thou didst lie
After, enabled but to suck and cry.
Think, when 'twas grown to most, 'twas a poor inn,
A province packed up in two yards of skin,
And that usurped or threatened with the rage
Of sicknesses, or their true mother, age.
But think that death hath now enfranchised thee, *Her liberty by*
Thou hast thy expansion now, and liberty; *death.*
Think that a rusty piece, discharged, is flown
In pieces, and the bullet is his own,
And freely flies; this to thy soul allow,
Think thy shell broke, think thy soul hatched but now.
And think this slow-paced soul, which late did cleave
To a body, and went but by the body's leave,
Twenty, perchance, or thirty mile a day,
Dispatches in a minute all the way
'Twixt heaven, and earth: she stays not in the air,
To look what meteors there themselves prepare;
She carries no desire to know, nor sense,
Whether th' air's middle region be intense;
For th' element of fire, she doth not know,
Whether she passed by such a place or no;
She baits not at the moon, nor cares to try
Whether in that new world, men live and die.
Venus retards her not, to inquire, how she
Can, (being one star) Hesper, and Vesper be;
He that charmed Argus' eyes, sweet Mercury,

Works not on her, who now is grown all eye;
Who, if she meet the body of the sun,
Goes through, not staying till his course be run;
Who finds in Mars his camp, no corps of guard;
Nor is by Jove, nor by his father barred;
But ere she can consider how she went,
At once is at, and through the firmament.
And as these stars were but so many beads
Strung on one string, speed undistinguished leads
Her through those spheres, as through the beads, a string,
Whose quick succession makes it still one thing:
As doth the pith, which, lest our bodies slack,
Strings fast the little bones of neck, and back;
So by the soul doth death string heaven and earth;
For when our soul enjoys this her third birth,
(Creation gave her one, a second, grace),
Heaven is as near, and present to her face,
As colours are, and objects, in a room
Where darkness was before, when tapers come.
This must, my soul, thy long-short progress be;
To advance these thoughts, remember then, that she,
She, whose fair body no such prison was,
But that a soul might well be pleased to pass
An age in her; she whose rich beauty lent
Mintage to others' beauties, for they went
But for so much as they were like to her;
She, in whose body (if we dare prefer
This low world, to so high a mark as she),
The western treasure, eastern spicery,
Europe, and Afric, and the unknown rest
Were easily found, or what in them was best;
And when we'have made this large discovery
Of all in her some one part, then will be
Twenty such parts, whose plenty and riches is

Enough to make twenty such worlds as this;
She, whom had they known who did first betroth
The tutelar angels, and assigned one, both
To nations, cities, and to companies,
To functions, offices, and dignities,
And to each several man, to him, and him,
They would have given her one for every limb;
She, of whose soul if we may say, 'twas gold,
Her body was th' electrum, and did hold
Many degrees of that; we understood
Her by her sight, her pure and eloquent blood
Spoke in her cheeks, and so distinctly wrought,
That one might almost say, her body thought;
She, she, thus richly and largely housed, is gone:
And chides us slow-paced snails who crawl upon
Our prison's prison, earth, nor think us well,
Longer, than whilst we bear our brittle shell.
. . . .
Thou art too narrow, wretch, to comprehend
Even thyself; yea though thou wouldst but bend
To know thy body. Have not all souls thought
For many ages, that our body is wrought
Of air, and fire, and other elements?
And now they think of new ingredients,
And one soul thinks one, and another way
Another thinks, and 'tis an even lay.
Know'st thou but how the stone doth enter in
The bladder's cave, and never break the skin?
Know'st thou how blood, which to the heart doth flow,
Doth from one ventricle to th' other go?
And for the putrid stuff, which thou dost spit,
Know'st thou how thy lungs have attracted it?
There are no passages, so that there is
(For aught thou know'st) piercing of substances.

And of those many opinions which men raise
Of nails and hairs, dost thou know which to praise?
What hope have we to know our selves, when we
Know not the least things, which for our use be?
We see in authors, too stiff to recant,
A hundred controversies of an ant;
And yet one watches, starves, freezes, and sweats,
To know but catechisms and alphabets
Of unconcerning things, matters of fact;
How others on our stage their parts did act;
What Caesar did, yea, and what Cicero said.
Why grass is green, or why our blood is red,
Are mysteries which none have reached unto.
In this low form, poor soul, what wilt thou do?
When wilt thou shake off this pedantery,
Of being taught by sense, and fantasy?
Thou look'st through spectacles; small things seem great
Below; but up unto the watch-tower get,
And see all things despoiled of fallacies:
Thou shalt not peep through lattices of eyes,
Nor hear through labyrinths of ears, nor learn
By circuit, or collections to discern.
In heaven thou straight know'st all, concerning it,
And what concerns it not, shalt straight forget.
. . . .
Up, up, my drowsy soul, where thy new ear
Shall in the angels' songs no discord hear;
Where thou shalt see the blessed mother-maid
Joy in not being that, which men have said.
Where she is exalted more for being good,
Than for her interest of motherhood.
Up to those patriarchs, which did longer sit
Expecting Christ, than they'have enjoyed him yet.
Up to those prophets, which now gladly see

Their prophecies grown to be history.
Up to th' apostles, who did bravely run
All the sun's course, with more light than the sun.
Up to those martyrs, who did calmly bleed
Oil to th' apostles' lamps, dew to their seed.
Up to those virgins, who thought that almost
They made joint tenants with the Holy Ghost,
If they to any should his temple give.
Up, up, for in that squadron there doth live
She, who hath carried thither new degrees
(As to their number) to their dignities.
She, who being to herself a State, enjoyed
All royalties which any State employed;
For she made wars, and triumphed; reason still
Did not o'erthrow, but rectify her will:
And she made peace, for no peace is like this,
That beauty and chastity together kiss:
She did high justice, for she crucified
Every first motion of rebellious pride:
And she gave pardons, and was liberal,
For, only herself except, she pardoned all:
She coined, in this, that her impressions gave
To all our actions all the worth they have:
She gave protections; the thoughts of her breast
Satan's rude officers could ne'er arrest.
As these prerogatives being met in one,
Made her a sovereign State, religion
Made her a Church; and these two made her all.
. . . .
But since all honours from inferiors flow,
(For they do give it; princes do but show
Whom they would have so honoured) and that this
On such opinions, and capacities
Is built, as rise, and fall, to more and less:

Alas, 'tis but a casual happiness.
Hath ever any man to' himself assigned
This or that happiness to arrest his mind,
But that another man, which takes a worse,
Thinks him a fool for having ta'en that course?
They who did labour Babel's tower to erect,
Might have considered, that for that effect,
All this whole solid earth could not allow
Nor furnish forth materials enow;
And that this centre, to raise such a place,
Was far too little, to have been the base;
No more affords this world, foundation
To erect true joy, were all the means in one.
. . . .
Here in a place, where mis-devotion frames   *Conclusion.*
A thousand prayers to saints, whose very names
The ancient Church knew not, heaven knows not yet,
And where, what laws of poetry admit,
Laws of religion have at least the same,
Immortal maid, I might invoke thy name.
Could any saint provoke that appetite,
Thou here shouldst make me a French convertite.
But thou wouldst not; nor wouldst thou be content,
To take this, for my second year's true rent,
Did this coin bear any other stamp, than his,
That gave thee power to do, me, to say this.
Since his will is, that to posterity,
Thou shouldst for life, and death, a pattern be,
And that the world should notice have of this,
The purpose, and th' authority is his;
Thou art the proclamation; and I am
The trumpet, at whose voice the people came.

III. DIVINE POEMS

6

This is my play's last scene, here heavens appoint
My pilgrimage's last mile; and my race
Idly, yet quickly run, hath this last pace,
My span's last inch, my minute's latest point,
And gluttonous death, will instantly unjoint
My body, and soul, and I shall sleep a space,
But my'ever-waking part shall see that face,
Whose fear already shakes my every joint:
Then, as my soul, to heaven her first seat, takes flight,
And earth-born body, in the earth shall dwell,
So, fall my sins, that all may have their right,
To where they are bred, and would press me, to hell.
Impute me righteous, thus purged of evil,
For thus I leave the world, the flesh, and devil.

7

At the round earth's imagined corners, blow
Your trumpets, angels, and arise, arise
From death, you numberless infinities
Of souls, and to your scattered bodies go,
All whom the flood did, and fire shall o'erthrow,
All whom war, dearth, age, agues, tyrannies,
Despair, law, chance, hath slain, and you whose eyes,
Shall behold God, and never taste death's woe.
But let them sleep, Lord, and me mourn a space,

For, if above all these, my sins abound,
'Tis late to ask abundance of thy grace,
When we are there; here on this lowly ground,
Teach me how to repent; for that's as good
As if thou hadst sealed my pardon, with thy blood.

9

If poisonous minerals, and if that tree,
Whose fruit threw death on else immortal us,
If lecherous goats, if serpents envious
Cannot be damned; alas, why should I be?
Why should intent or reason, born in me,
Make sins, else equal, in me more heinous?
And mercy being easy, and glorious
To God, in his stern wrath, why threatens he?
But who am I, that dare dispute with thee
O God? Oh! of thine only worthy blood,
And my tears, make a heavenly lethean flood,
And drown in it my sin's black memory;
That thou remember them, some claim as debt,
I think it mercy, if thou wilt forget.

10

Death be not proud, though some have called thee
Mighty and dreadful, for, thou art not so,
For, those, whom thou think'st, thou dost overthrow,
Die not, poor death, nor yet canst thou kill me;
From rest and sleep, which but thy pictures be,
Much pleasure, then from thee, much more must flow,
And soonest our best men with thee do go,
Rest of their bones, and soul's delivery.
Thou art slave to fate, chance, kings, and desperate men,

And dost with poison, war, and sickness dwell,
And poppy, or charms can make us sleep as well,
And better than thy stroke; why swell'st thou then?
One short sleep past, we wake eternally,
And death shall be no more, Death thou shalt die.

13

What if this present were the world's last night?
Mark in my heart, O soul, where thou dost dwell,
The picture of Christ crucified, and tell
Whether that countenance can thee affright,
Tears in his eyes quench the amazing light,
Blood fills his frowns, which from his pierced head fell,
And can that tongue adjudge thee unto hell,
Which prayed forgiveness for his foes' fierce spite?
No, no; but as in my idolatry
I said to all my profane mistresses,
Beauty, of pity, foulness only is
A sign of rigour: so I say to thee,
To wicked spirits are horrid shapes assigned,
This beauteous form assures a piteous mind.

14

Batter my heart, three-personed God; for, you
As yet but knock, breathe, shine, and seek to mend;
That I may rise, and stand, o'erthrow me, and bend
Your force, to break, blow, burn, and make me new.
I, like an usurped town, to another due,
Labour to admit you, but oh, to no end,
Reason your viceroy in me, me should defend,
But is captived, and proves weak or untrue,
Yet dearly'I love you, and would be loved fain,

But am betrothed unto your enemy,
Divorce me, untie, or break that knot again,
Take me to you, imprison me, for I
Except you enthral me, never shall be free,
Nor ever chaste, except you ravish me.

17

Since she whom I loved hath paid her last debt
To nature, and to hers, and my good is dead,
And her soul early into heaven ravished,
Wholly in heavenly things my mind is set.
Here the admiring her my mind did whet
To seek thee God; so streams do show the head,
But though I have found thee, and thou my thirst hast fed,
A holy thirsty dropsy melts me yet.
But why should I beg more love, when as thou
Dost woo my soul for hers; offering all thine:
And dost not only fear lest I allow
My love to saints and angels, things divine,
But in thy tender jealousy dost doubt
Lest the world, flesh, yea Devil put thee out.

18

Show me dear Christ, thy spouse, so bright and clear.
What, is it she, which on the other shore
Goes richly painted? or which robbed and tore
Laments and mourns in Germany and here?
Sleeps she a thousand, then peeps up one year?
Is she self truth and errs? now new, now outwore?
Doth she, and did she, and shall she evermore
On one, on seven, or on no hill appear?
Dwells she with us, or like adventuring knights

First travail we to seek and then make love?
Betray kind husband thy spouse to our sights,
And let mine amorous soul court thy mild dove,
Who is most true, and pleasing to thee, then
When she' is embraced and open to most men.

19

Oh, to vex me, contraries meet in one:
Inconstancy unnaturally hath begot
A constant habit; that when I would not
I change in vows, and in devotion.
As humorous is my contrition
As my profane love, and as soon forgot:
As riddlingly distempered, cold and hot,
As praying, as mute; as infinite, as none.
I durst not view heaven yesterday; and today
In prayers, and flattering speeches I court God:
Tomorrow I quake with true fear of his rod.
So my devout fits come and go away
Like a fantastic ague: save that here
Those are my best days, when I shake with fear.

Good Friday, 1613. Riding Westward

Let man's soul be a sphere, and then, in this,
The intelligence that moves, devotion is,
And as the other spheres, by being grown
Subject to foreign motions, lose their own,
And being by others hurried every day,
Scarce in a year their natural form obey:
Pleasure or business, so, our souls admit
For their first mover, and are whirled by it.

Hence is't, that I am carried towards the west
This day, when my soul's form bends toward the east.
There I should see a sun, by rising set,
And by that setting endless day beget;
But that Christ on this Cross, did rise and fall,
Sin had eternally benighted all.
Yet dare I' almost be glad, I do not see
That spectacle of too much weight for me.
Who sees God's face, that is self life, must die;
What a death were it then to see God die?
It made his own lieutenant Nature shrink,
It made his footstool crack, and the sun wink.
Could I behold those hands which span the poles,
And turn all spheres at once, pierced with those holes?
Could I behold that endless height which is
Zenith to us, and to'our antipodes,
Humbled below us? or that blood which is
The seat of all our souls, if not of his,
Made dirt of dust, or that flesh which was worn,
By God, for his apparel, ragged, and torn?
If on these things I durst not look, durst I
Upon his miserable mother cast mine eye,
Who was God's partner here, and furnished thus
Half of that sacrifice, which ransomed us?
Though these things, as I ride, be from mine eye,
They are present yet unto my memory,
For that looks towards them; and thou look'st towards me,
O Saviour, as thou hang'st upon the tree;
I turn my back to thee, but to receive
Corrections, till thy mercies bid thee leave.
O think me worth thine anger, punish me,
Burn off my rusts, and my deformity,
Restore thine image, so much, by thy grace,
That thou mayst know me, and I'll turn my face.

Resurrection, imperfect

Sleep sleep old sun, thou canst not have repassed
As yet, the wound thou took'st on Friday last;
Sleep then, and rest; the world may bear thy stay,
A better sun rose before thee today,
Who, not content to enlighten all that dwell
On the earth's face, as thou, enlightened hell,
And made the dark fires languish in that vale,
As, at thy presence here, our fires grow pale.
Whose body having walked on earth, and now
Hasting to heaven, would, that he might allow
Himself unto all stations, and fill all,
For these three days become a mineral;
He was all gold when he lay down, but rose
All tincture, and doth not alone dispose
Leaden and iron wills to good, but is
Of power to make even sinful flesh like his.
Had one of those, whose credulous piety
Thought, that a soul one might discern and see
Go from a body, at this sepulchre been,
And, issuing from the sheet, this body seen,
He would have justly thought this body a soul,
If not of any man, yet of the whole.
Desunt caetera.

From *The Lamentations of Jeremy*

CHAPTER 5

Remember, O Lord, what is fallen on us;
  See, and mark how we are reproached thus,

For unto strangers our possession
    Is turned, our houses unto aliens gone,

Our mothers are become as widows, we
    As orphans all, and without father be;
Waters which are our own, we drink, and pay,
    And upon our own wood a price they lay.

Our persecutors on our necks do sit,
    They make us travail, and not intermit,
We stretch our hands unto th' Egyptians
    To get us bread; and to the Assyrians.

Our fathers did these sins, and are no more,
    But we do bear the sins they did before.
They are but servants, which do rule us thus,
    Yet from their hands none would deliver us.

With danger of our life our bread we gat;
    For in the wilderness, the sword did wait.
The tempests of this famine we lived in,
    Black as an oven coloured had our skin:

In Judah's cities they the maids abused
    By force, and so women in Sion used.
The princes with their hands they hung; no grace
    Nor honour gave they to the Elder's face.

Unto the mill our young men carried are,
    And children fall under the wood they bear.
Elders, the gates; youth did their songs forbear,
    Gone was our joy; our dancings, mournings were.

Now is the crown fall'n from our head; and woe
    Be unto us, because we'have sinned so.
For this our hearts do languish, and for this
    Over our eyes a cloudy dimness is.

Because Mount Sion desolate doth lie,
    And foxes there do go at liberty:
But thou O Lord art ever, and thy throne
    From generation, to generation.

Why shouldst thou forget us eternally?
    Or leave us thus long in this misery?
Restore us Lord to thee, that so we may
    Return, and as of old, renew our day.

For oughtest thou, O Lord, despise us thus,
    And to be utterly enraged at us?

A Hymn to Christ, at the Author's last going into Germany

In what torn ship soever I embark,
That ship shall be my emblem of thy ark;
What sea soever swallow me, that flood
Shall be to me an emblem of thy blood;
Though thou with clouds of anger do disguise
Thy face; yet through that mask I know those eyes,
    Which, though they turn away sometimes,
        They never will despise.

I sacrifice this Island unto thee,
And all whom I loved there, and who loved me;
When I have put our seas 'twixt them and me,
Put thou thy sea betwixt my sins and thee.

As the tree's sap doth seek the root below
In winter, in my winter now I go,
    Where none but thee, th' eternal root
        Of true love I may know.

Nor thou nor thy religion dost control,
The amorousness of an harmonious soul,
But thou wouldst have that love thyself: as thou
Art jealous, Lord, so I am jealous now,
Thou lov'st not, till from loving more, thou free
My soul; who ever gives, takes liberty:
    O, if thou car'st not whom I love
        Alas, thou lov'st not me.

Seal then this bill of my divorce to all,
On whom those fainter beams of love did fall;
Marry those loves, which in youth scattered be
On fame, wit, hopes (false mistresses) to thee.
Churches are best for prayer, that have least light:
To see God only, I go out of sight:
    And to 'scape stormy days, I choose
        An everlasting night.

Hymn to God my God, in my Sickness

Since I am coming to that holy room,
    Where, with thy choir of saints for evermore,
I shall be made thy music; as I come
    I tune the instrument here at the door,
    And what I must do then, think here before.

Whilst my physicians by their love are grown
    Cosmographers, and I their map, who lie

Flat on this bed, that by them may be shown
    That this is my south-west discovery
    Per fretum febris, by these straits to die,

I joy, that in these straits, I see my west;
    For, though their currents yield return to none,
What shall my west hurt me? As west and east
    In all flat maps (and I am one) are one,
    So death doth touch the resurrection.

Is the Pacific Sea my home? Or are
    The eastern riches? Is Jerusalem?
Anyan, and Magellan, and Gibraltar,
    All straits, and none but straits, are ways to them,
    Whether where Japhet dwelt, or Cham, or Shem.

We think that Paradise and Calvary,
    Christ's Cross, and Adam's tree, stood in one place;
Look Lord, and find both Adams met in me;
    As the first Adam's sweat surrounds my face,
    May the last Adam's blood my soul embrace.

So, in his purple wrapped receive me Lord,
    By these his thorns give me his other crown;
And as to others' souls I preached thy word,
    Be this my text, my sermon to mine own,
    Therefore that he may raise the Lord throws down.

A Hymn to God the Father

I

Wilt thou forgive that sin where I begun,
    Which was my sin, though it were done before?

Wilt thou forgive that sin, through which I run,
  And do run still: though still I do deplore?
    When thou hast done, thou hast not done,
      For, I have more.

II

Wilt thou forgive that sin which I have won
  Others to sin? and, made my sin their door?
Wilt thou forgive that sin which I did shun
  A year, or two: but wallowed in, a score?
    When thou hast done, thou hast not done,
      For I have more.

III

I have a sin of fear, that when I have spun
  My last thread, I shall perish on the shore;
But swear by thy self, that at my death thy son
  Shall shine as he shines now, and heretofore;
    And, having done that, thou hast done,
      I fear no more.

Glossary

Unfamiliar, puzzling, and occasionally misleading terms in the poems of Donne most often have to do with theology, with medicine, and in particular with the practice of alchemy. As nowadays defined, this amalgam of chemistry with philosophy had as its aims the transmutation of base metals into gold and the discovery of a universal cure, the elixir of life. Just how seriously those aims were taken may be suggested by the following, from a lecture by John Maynard Keynes (as quoted by Freeman Dyson in Disturbing the Universe*) on the unpublished writings of Isaac Newton: "A large section . . . related to alchemy—transmutation, the philosopher's stone, the elixir of life. All his unpublished works on esoteric and theological matters are marked by careful learning, accurate method, and extreme sobriety of statement. They are just as sane as the 'Principia,' if their whole matter and purpose were not magical." By the seventeenth century the word* alchemy *had nevertheless acquired a secondary meaning denoting an imposture, and Donne sometimes used it in that sense.*

Actives and passives Those who, as lovers, make the first advance and those who respond to it.

Ague Malarial fever, often accompanied by fits of shivering.

Alchemy See headnote to this glossary.

Allay Alloy, i.e., a mixture or solution; also, anything added that lowers value or purity.

Anachorit *See* **Anchorite.**

Anatomy A dissection; a detailed examination or analysis.

Anchorite A person who has gone into seclusion for religious reasons (also *Anachorit*).

Angel In medieval theology, an immortal, spiritual being attendant on the deity. In the celestial hierarchy of such beings the angels occupied the lowest order; above them, in ascending rank, were archangels, principalities, powers, virtues, dominations or dominions, thrones, cherubim, and seraphim. Also, a gold coin bearing the figure of an angel.

Angelica In Ariosto's *Orlando Furioso,* a heroine who several times escapes her quarreling suitors.

Anyan An imaginary strait, the presumed northwest passage from the Atlantic to the Pacific.

Argus In Greek mythology, a giant with eyes all over his body, whom Hera employed as a spy.

Ascapart A giant thirty feet high.

Aspen (adjective) Shivering or trembling like the leaves of an aspen tree.

Atlanta (or **Atalanta**) In Greek mythology, Atalanta was distracted from her race with Hippomanes, whom she refused to marry unless he could outrun her, by three golden apples thrown down by Aphrodite.

Atomy (from Greek *atomos,* indivisible) A particle; a component.

Bajazet In Marlowe's *Tamburlaine,* the emperor of the Turks, who was shut up in a wooden cage.

Balm In medieval medicine, a vital substance believed to pervade all organic beings. Donne referred to it in a letter as a "natural inborn preservative." Also, an aromatic oil or unguent, such as is used in the sacrament of extreme unction.

Bench Court of the Queen's Bench, one of the inns of court.

Benight To cloud or darken.

Beza A French Calvinist theologian.

Bill A halberd; a legal petition; an order to pay. *See also* **Plaguy bill.**

Brave Possessing or displaying courage; also, making a fine display; splendid.

Busk Corset.

Calenture A tropical fever; it sometimes caused sailors, in their delirium, to leap into the sea.

Capuchin One of an order of monks vowed to absolute poverty.

Carrack A Spanish merchant vessel. The *Great Carrack* was captured with a load of pepper in 1592.

Carthusian Pertaining to an order of contemplative monks noted for their austerity (from Chartreuse, where the order was founded).

Chaos The disordered state of unformed matter believed to have existed before the creation of the universe.

Charing Cross Originally, a large cross erected by Edward I.

Cheapside A market district in London.

Chemic An alchemist.

Cochineal A vivid red dye made from the bodies of a species of tropical insects and used in cosmetics.

Concoction In alchemy, the process of sublimation or purification.

Correctives Drugs intended to restore balance within the body. *See also* **Galenist; Humor.**

Covetize An immoderate desire.

Cozen To cheat or deceive.

Crab A reference to the constellation Cancer, the sign of the zodiac under which the summer solstice occurs.

Desunt caetera Latin, "the rest is missing."

Divorcement A separation

Domination *See* **Angel.**

Dross An impurity discarded in the process of concoction.

Ecstasy A state in which the normal understanding is said to be surpassed. Donne himself, in a letter, called it "a departing, and secession, and suspension of the soul."

Electrum An alloy of gold and silver.

Elements The fundamental constituents of the universe. In ancient and medieval cosmology, these were earth, air, water, and fire.

Elixir In alchemy, a substance believed to have the power to transmute base metals. The elixir of life, or panacea, was believed capable of healing all diseases.

Express An alchemical term, meaning to extract.

Fable In "The Calm," a reference to Aesop's fable of King Log and King Stork.

Firmament In the Ptolemaic cosmology, the regions above the moon, which were regarded as fixed and immutable.

Galenist A physician in the tradition of Galen, whose aim was to correct an excess in the body of one of the four humors. *See* **Humor.**

Goat A reference to the constellation Capricorn, under whose sign the winter solstice occurs.

Grogaram A grosgrain fabric.

Hilary A court term at the beginning of the calendar year.

Hilliard, Nicholas A court painter noted for his miniature portraits.

Home-meats Domestic gossip.

Humor In medieval physiology, one of the four fluids of the body: blood, phlegm, choler, and black bile. The fluid that tended to dominate was thought to determine one's character and health.

Hydroptic Dropsical; immoderately thirsty.

Idiot (adjective) Ignorant.

Indias The East Indies, regarded as the source of perfumes and spices; the West Indies, regarded as the source of gold and other minerals.

Ingenuity Ingenuousness.

Intelligence In medieval cosmology, the heavenly bodies were thought to consist of a sphere and an intelligence seated within it and controlling its motions.

Jonas The prophet Jonah, who was blamed by mariners for causing a storm at sea.

Lanthorns Used by a fleet for maintaining contact by night, but useless when the ships are not moving, as in "The Calm."

Lethe In classical mythology, the river of forgetfulness.

Limbeck Alembic, an apparatus used in alchemy for distilling.

Line The equator.

Lucy, Saint (from *lux,* Latin for light) Her feast day, December 13, was thought to coincide with the shortest day of the year.

Lunatic (from the Latin *luna*) Having to do with the moon; hence, denoting one who is changeable or inconstant as well as mentally deranged.

Macaron A fop who is also stupid.

Mandrake A plant with narcotic properties, whose root had a quasi-human shape, and which was thought to utter a shriek as it was pulled from the ground.

Manna The food miraculously provided to the Israelites in the desert.

Mechanic (adjective) Low, as of one who performs manual labor.

Meteors Atmospheric phenomena occurring in the lower air. (*Meteorology* derives from this meaning of the word.)

Mithridate An antidote for all poisons, having many ingredients.

Moschite A mosque.

Nocturnal (noun) In the Catholic liturgy, a night office or vigil.

Non obstante Waiving of a law in favor of an individual.

Orithea In Greek mythology, a nymph pursued by Boreas, god of the north wind.

Panurge In the novels of Rabelais, a character who knew a dozen languages.

Paradise In medieval theology, the abode of the righteous after death. The Mahometan paradise was envisioned as a place of unending carnal pleasure. The idea of a walled park or garden is implicit in the Old Iranian *pairi-daēza,* from which the word is originally derived.

Passives *See* **Actives and passives.**

Pater Noster The Christian prayer beginning "Our Father who art in heaven."

Per fretum febris Latin for "through the strait of fever"—an allusion to the voyage through the Strait of Magellan.

Philosophy Natural science; as in "new philosophy," a reference to the theories of Copernicus, Kepler, and Galileo, which placed the sun at the center of the universe.

Physic A drug used for medicinal purposes.

Piece A firearm.

Pinnace A light sailing vessel.

Plaguy bill An obituary list, posted weekly during outbreaks of plague.

Pleas The Court of Common Pleas.

Powder Gunpowder.

Pox Syphilis, which first devastated Europe in the fifteenth century.

Progress A royal journey.

Pursuivant One officially employed to search out concealed Roman Catholics, especially priests and Jesuits in disguise.

Quintessence The pure essence of anything. A reputed fifth element in addition to earth, air, water, and fire.

Rash A smooth silk fabric.

Ravish To violate; also, to carry away or overwhelm.

Relic A corpse, or the buried remains of one.

Remorse A feeling of pity or compassion.

Saint Lucy *See* **Lucy, Saint.**

Schedule A supplement appended to a document.

Sclavonians Slavs.

Seven Sleepers In medieval lore, seven Christian youths who fled from persecution, were walled up in the cave where they had hidden, and miraculously slept there for 187 years.

Size Assize, a session of court.

Spectacles Artificial means of seeing, such as mirrors or telescopes.

Specular stone A legendary building material noted for its transparency and the skill required to work it; possibly a reference to selenite.

Sphere In Ptolemaic astronomy, one of a series of concentric, transparent, revolving globes, each containing one of the planets, with the earth at the center. The music of these turning bodies was regarded as the perfect concord.

Spirit In medieval physiology, a substance within the blood which was believed to govern the body and its parts.

Spittal A hospital, particularly one for sufferers of venereal disease.

Spleen In the medieval physiology of humors, this organ was regarded as the seat of black bile or melancholy.

Squib A firecracker.

Subtle Fine or rarefied, as well as not easily comprehended.

Throughly Thoroughly.

Tincture The quintessential principle within a substance.

Torpedo A fish capable of giving an electric shock that had a numbing effect.

Transubstantiate To transform one substance into another. In Christian theology, to change the substance of the Eucharistic bread and wine into the presence of Christ.

Tricesimo The thirtieth year of the reign of Elizabeth I (1588).

Tufftaffaty A thin, glossy, tufted silk.

Urim and Thummin In the Old Testament, gems empowering the wearer to speak with authority.

Valediction A farewell utterance.

Venite (Latin imperative, "Come") A summons, as to the Last Judgment.

Vestal A virgin consecrated to serving the Roman goddess Vesta, guardian of the hearth.

Wittol One who sanctions, or connives in, his wife's adultery.

Worthies Nine heroes, beginning with Hector, renowned for their bravery. *See* **Brave.**

Xerxes King of the Persians. His "strange Lydian love" is a reference to his admiration for a plane tree in Lydia, whose size was indicative of great age.

About the Editor

❖❖

Amy Clampitt was born and brought up in rural Iowa, and graduated from Grinnell College. She has since lived mainly in New York City, where most of her career has been spent in and around book publishing, with a seven-year stint as a reference librarian for the National Audubon Society. In 1978 she began publishing poems in magazines, and in 1982 was awarded a Guggenheim Fellowship. Her three full-length collections of poetry are The Kingfisher *(1983),* What the Light Was Like *(1985), and* Archaic Figure *(1987). She has been Writer in Residence at the College of William and Mary and Visiting Writer at Amherst College. She is a fellow of the Academy of American Poets and a member of the Institute of the American Academy and Institute of Arts and Letters. In June 1987 she was Phi Beta Kappa Poet at the Harvard Literary Exercises.*